The Player, The Rapture, The New Age

Novels by Michael Tolkin

The Player
Among the Dead

The Player,
The Rapture,
The New Age

Three Screenplays

by Michael Tolkin

Grove Press
New York

Published simultaneously in Canada
Printed in the United States of America

FIRST EDITION

Library of Congress Cataloging-in-Publication Data

Tolkin, Michael.
    The player; The rapture; The new age: three screenplays /
    Michael Tolkin. — 1st ed.
      ISBN 0-8021-3392-4
      1. Motion picture plays.   I. Title.   II. Title: Player.
    III. Title: Rapture.   IV. Title: New age.
    PS3570.04278P56   1994 812'.54—dc20   94-1255

Grove Press
841 Broadway
New York, NY 10003

10 9 8 7 6 5 4 3 2

It's customary and impossible to offer some acknowledgments to those who helped make these movies. If their names are in the credits, I have reason to thank them, and if I shorten the list to four or five people from each film to whom particular thanks are due, another ten will feel justifiably slighted.

Each of these movies has its angels. *The Rapture* began after long conversations with my brother, Stephen, and without him, I wouldn't have Sharon's complaint at the end. *The Player* is a movie because David Brown wouldn't leave me alone. Oliver Stone and Arnon Milchan made *The New Age* possible, but because his name belongs on every list, this book is dedicated to Nick Wechsler.

The poem is a capsule where we wrap up our punishable secrets. And as they confine in themselves the only "life," the ability to sprout at a more favorable time, to come true in their secret structure to the very minutest details of our thoughts, so they get their specific virtue.

We write for this, that the seed come true.

from The Autobiography of William Carlos Williams

Contents

The Player, The Rapture, The New Age

Introduction

The scripts in this book conform to the films as released. Some writers, given the chance to publish their scripts, go back to earlier drafts, to give readers a chance to see how the movies changed from their original intentions, but the issue of original intention isn't so simple as reaching to the shelf and taking down the draft with the earliest date, as though the first draft is the purest draft, the true draft. Early drafts are like one of those children's flip books divided into thirds; they're beasts with devil faces, angel wings, and duck feet.

There is no such beast as an original version. Is the original draft the one shown to the agent and producer, or the draft that everyone agrees is right to show "the money," or is it the draft that raised the money, or rather, is it the draft that got the money interested, or the draft the studio asked for before they'd commit? You might say that the draft that went out for money would be the one to publish, since that version, having no concessions to budget, represents the writer's fullest vision; but adjusting a script for the reality of the available money brings the writer into other aspects of reality, focusing him on the essentials of the story, which usually makes a better story.

Maybe the draft the writer is happiest with is the best one to call the original draft, but if the writer's happiness is a criterion and the writer cringes when scenes he thought were magic die on the screen in the film's earliest assemblies, what does it serve to publish them, after they're cut from the movie? Some scenes seem necessary in the script because we read logically, but when we see a movie we usually make brilliant leaps ahead of the writer, and the scene that says what the audience already knows is not necessarily something that should have been cut from the script before production; scripts need explanations that movies don't.

The draft that went to the actors might be great, but then things change in rehearsal when the actors bring themselves to the parts, so maybe the draft that goes to the set is the draft that shows the intentions against which the movie can be properly compared. But the draft that goes to the set is changed by the set, and since the movie was written for the set and the camera, refusing to publish a transcription of the movie because it doesn't live up to the screenplay is blaming the meat of reality for obscuring the ether of an idea, which puts reality—which puts life—in a state of terrible theological disrepute.

Also, involving the audience in the steps of the film's progress makes detached experts of everyone, which is another disaster. A scene comes along in a film, and with too much information we're suddenly thinking about the history of the scene, and the film is destroyed until we come back to it. Those directors who participate in the critical dissection of their films by adding outtakes and cut scenes to their laser discs hurt themselves and hurt their movies. We did this with *The Player;* one of the audio tracks has our commentary on each scene. It's funny, but it's easy. The work then becomes something that the audience is invited to view with superiority, a puzzle to be deciphered, when the work should stand in opposition to its own analysis and, in turn, decipher the viewer. The best books, the best movies read us, watch us, and as we come to love and understand the work, or even run from it, we discover ourselves. When people talk about interactivity all I can think of is the Roman crowd giving thumbs up or down. The audience does not create, and the propaganda surrounding the supposed interactive future is filled with lies about audience control. It's all pinball; it's just that with the computer you're inside the machine, so you don't see the outside of the frame.

But this is really a cover for the reason I glided over at the beginning: I know that every script I wrote had something I shouldn't have given up, and people read closely, and I don't want to be asked why some jewels were tossed aside. If I say forthrightly, "Well, I cut that scene because I was stupid," I'll be hanging myself. Instead of telling the truth—that I may have been wrong—I pretend to an intellectual astringency and say that one has to accept one's story, the inspiration as it comes, and the way it finds expression, and finally, the way the world receives it. The movies changed as they went from first notes and outline through the final cut because they did, because for better or worse those of us who made the films were chasing something, and the obsessions denied for fear of the paths they lead to, which sometimes land you on the far side of town from the bank, are better pursued than abandoned. The blocked imperative kills. I hope that sounds reasonably philosophical. It's the kind of thought that's given in routine defense of art, and it may also be the great defense of wickedness, if the artist as blind hero is the favored model. The truth is more complicated. Sometimes a good idea is lost for bad reasons. One sequence we shot for *The Rapture* was ruined by a scratched negative. The scene that replaced it may be better, but then I have to say that, or thank providence, because I think it's better to look back on a completed film as what was intended, especially when something comes up that doesn't work. There is no one to blame but yourself.

Another reason not to publish early drafts is that some of those lost scenes might show up somewhere else, in other movies. I can just imagine going to a screening of a film with one of those scenes and finding the guys who subscribe to *Premiere* all whispering to their dates, "As it happens, that scene was originally written for *The Player*." What does that help? Is it generous or clever? There's some dialogue from *The New Age* that never made it to the screen, and I know it's going to show up somewhere else, and if I print it here, then it just serves some pointless anecdote down the line.

And another reason . . . no, there's no reason to continue in this vein. Instead, I have this thought that I've been trying to squeeze into this piece, and I don't know where to put it. So I'll just put it here: Say that Fassbinder is your hero, but you want to get rich, so instead you copy George Lucas. You're doomed, unless you can bring what you love about Fassbinder into what you love about Lucas, and then only if you really also love Lucas and understand what you love. People usually steal the wrong gifts from their gods. The most important thing to learn from John Ford isn't the composition of his gunfights, but the sense of sympathy that leads to the composition.

In this volume, the only violation of the principle against publishing an early draft is the inclusion of my first real draft of *The Rapture,* twenty-two pages long, which I wanted to make as a short subject. Nick Wechsler promised that if I expanded the script to the length of a feature he would find the money, so I did. The movie has its fans, and I thought they'd like to see how it began.

Beyond this, I don't think it's a good idea to say too much else about these movies; it's still early, and it's best just to let them have their own life, without my reviews of them. Peter Weller told me that Sidney Lumet told him that if you hated making the movies but the reviews are good, don't forget what you really felt; and if making the movie was a great event but the reviews are bad, don't forget that either. I was fortunate, I worked with nobles: Mimi Rogers, David Duchovny, Kimberley Cullum, Patrick Bauchau, Peter Weller, and Judy Davis, and all the others, all the day players who stayed up late and were paid badly. I'm thinking of Patrick Dollaghan, who played the swinger executive in *The Rapture* and ad-libbed my favorite line. Bauchau has found a swinger couple at an airport bar and brought them back to his house for an orgy with Mimi Rogers. Dollaghan shakes the ice in his glass and says, "Here's to open-minded people and L.A. My kind of town." In *The New Age* he pops in as Peter and Judy's store is dying, when everything is for sale at 70 percent off. When he's at the cash register with a sweater for his girlfriend, Peter asks him how he's going to pay and he says, "Plastic," and the way he says it kills me every time I see the film, because all the horror of the world is in the empty swagger of his delivery. As Adam West walks away from Peter Weller after giving him a bad check, he snaps his fingers to the music, and that snap kills me too, because it's perfect, because it's the gesture of a man pretending to be what he is, because it's worth burying in a time capsule to show the future what bodies did the year that fathers bounced checks on their sons. Those moments make me as happy as watching all of David Lean's extras taking no prisoners. Sometimes the great moments that others come up with aren't in dialogue or action. Robin Standefer, the production designer on *The Rapture* and *The New Age,* found a creepy Patrick Nagel print for Mimi's apartment, and I didn't know how right that choice was, how accurate, until two years later, when I saw almost the same print in a real swinger's house that I was looking at on a location scout for *The New Age.* Is that the world as will and representation? We always said we were making period pictures set in the present.

These are three movies about California between 1990 and 1994. So many movies are shot here arbitrarily, and I wanted to be specific. The films have their partisans and enemies, but when the question of sympathy for some of the characters comes up, when people turn from the films because they don't like the characters, I just want to offer them this story from the life of Jackie Gleason. Someone asked him, "Jackie, how come you drink a fifth of scotch a day?" And Jackie said, "I don't drink to get rid of *my* warts, I drink to get rid of *yours.*"

And if that doesn't work, try this: I wish I could attribute the quote to Bukowski, but it was Strindberg, in his foreword to *Miss Julie,* who best expressed what a writer's position should be to his audience: "That my tragedy depresses many people is their own fault."

I suspect that with these films I've finished something, but what that is, I'm not yet sure.

The Player

(Based on the Novel)

Filmmakers

Directed by	Robert Altman
Screenplay by	Michael Tolkin
Executive Producer	Cary Brokaw
Producer	David Brown
Producer	Michael Tolkin
Producer	Nick Wechsler
Co-Producer	Scott Bushnell
Director of Photography	Jean Lepine
Editor	Geraldine Peroni
Production Designer	Stephen Altman
Music by	Thomas Newman

Cast

Griffin Mill	Tim Robbins
June Gudmundsdottir	Greta Scacchi
Walter Stuckel	Fred Ward
Detective Avery	Whoopi Goldberg
Larry Levy '	Peter Gallagher
Joel Levison	Brion James
Bonnie Sherow	Cynthia Stevenson
David Kahane	Vincent D'Onofrio
Andy Civella	Dean Stockwell
Tom Oakley	Richard E. Grant
Dick Mellen	Sydney Pollack
Detective De Longpre	Lyle Lovett
Celia	Dina Merrill
Jan	Angela Hall
Sandy	Leah Ayres
Jimmy Chase	Paul Hewitt
Reg Goldman	Randall Batinkoff
Steve Reeves	Jeremy Piven
Whitney Gersh	Gina Gershon
Frank Murphy	Frank Barhydt
Marty Grossman	Mike E. Kaplan
Gar Girard	Kevin Scannell
Witness	Margery Bond
Detective Broom	Susan Emshwiller
Phil	Brian Brophy
Eric Schecter	Michael Tolkin
Carl Schecter	Stephen Tolkin
Natalie	Natalie Strong
Walter	Pete Koch
Trixie	Pamela Bowen
Rocco	Jeff Weston

EXTERIOR: STUDIO. DAY.

Close-up: mural. The voice of an assistant director. The camera starts on C. Bragg mural of The Movie Queen.

> VOICE (*offscreen*): Quiet on the set! Scene one, take ten. Marker!

(*Slate in. We pull back from a motion picture slate to see* SANDY, *a secretary, reaching over her desk to answer the phone.*)

> VOICE (*offscreen*): And, action!

> SANDY: Joel Levison's office. No, I'm sorry, he's not in yet. May I take a message?

(CELIA, *an executive secretary, enters.*)

> SANDY (*still on phone*): Yes, Mr. Levy, I'll tell him you called.

> CELIA: You never say that. He's either in conference, in a meeting . . . He's always in. Now, who was that?

> SANDY: Larry Levy.

> CELIA: God, I hope there wasn't anything in the trades this morning, was there?

> SANDY: Well, I don't know. The mail's late.

> CELIA: Well, go get them. Now. I want them back here before he arrives.

(SANDY *is out from behind her desk and on her way running. The camera pans up the street as she runs toward the mail room. We pick up a Range Rover driving in. The camera follows it to a parking spot in front of the office. It is met by a writer,* ADAM SIMON, *as* GRIFFIN MILL, *a thirty-five-year-old studio executive, gets out of his car and goes into the main door of his office building.*)

> ADAM: Griffin, Griffin, hi, Griffin, hi, Adam Simon. I know we're not supposed to meet till next week—

> GRIFFIN: I didn't realize we were meeting next week.

> ADAM: Yeah, I just wanted to plant the seed in your head. Just now. Just so that we could, you know—

GRIFFIN: I'm booked up. I can't hear a pitch right now—
ADAM: Okay, but picture this, picture this. A planet in the far, far future. A planet with two suns—
GRIFFIN: Who plays the sons?
ADAM: No, no, suns, large solar discs—
GRIFFIN: Listen, you've got to run this idea past Bonnie Sherow.

(*The camera follows them to the bungalow door. As* GRIFFIN *and* ADAM *enter,* WALTER STUCKEL, *the head of studio security, and* JIMMY CHASE, *a studio gofer, leave the building. We follow them.* JIMMY *walks his bicycle.*)

WALTER: These pictures they make these days are all MTV. Cut, cut, cut, cut. The opening shot of Welles's *Touch of Evil* was six and a half minutes long.
JIMMY: Six and a half minutes, Walter?
WALTER: Three or four anyway. It set up the whole picture with that one tracking shot. My father was key grip on that shoot.
JIMMY: Hey, what about *Absolute Beginners?* That was an extraordinary shot.
WALTER: What the hell was that? I never heard of it.
JIMMY: Julian Temple. It's an English film.
WALTER: English. We're talking about American movies. And Orson Welles was the master.

(*They walk past Griffin's office window, and camera looks in to find* BUCK HENRY *sitting there as* JAN, *Griffin's secretary, gives him a cup of coffee.* GRIFFIN *enters his new office.*)

GRIFFIN: Pellegrino, please.
JAN: I've got Calistoga.
BUCK: Thank you much. (*To* GRIFFIN:) How are you?
GRIFFIN: Good, how you doing?

(JAN *exits and comes back with Calistoga for* GRIFFIN. GRIFFIN *sits at his desk.*)

BUCK: Good.
GRIFFIN: What do you got for me?
BUCK: Okay, here it is. *The Graduate,* part two.
GRIFFIN: Oh, good, good.

Buck: Now, listen. The three principals are still with us: Dustin Hoffman, Anne Bancroft, Katharine Ross— twenty-five years later, and so are the characters: Ben, Elaine, and Mrs. Robinson. Ben and Elaine are married. Still, they live in a big old spooky house in Northern California somewhere and Mrs. Robinson lives with them.

Griffin: Hmmm.

Buck: Her aging mother who has had a stroke—

Griffin: Mrs. Robinson had a stroke—

Buck: Mrs. Robinson had a stroke, so she can't talk.

Griffin: Is this going to be funny?

Buck: Yeah, it'll be funny—

Griffin: With a stroke?

Buck: Dark and weird and funny and with a stroke.

Griffin: Okay.

Buck: Maybe it's not a stroke, maybe it's, I don't know what—

Griffin: Anyway, go on.

Buck: It's a malady of some sorts.

Griffin: Okay.

Buck: She's up there in the bedroom upstairs listening to everything that happens. They've got a daughter who's just graduated from college—

Griffin: That's good, that's good. Young blood.

Buck: Twenty-two, twenty-three years old, like a . . . Julia Roberts—

Griffin (*simultaneous*): Julia Roberts, right.

Jan: Excuse me, what did you want me to do with these scripts?

Griffin: That goes to Bonnie Sherow, and find out from studio security how Adam Simon got on the lot. I want to know.

Jan: Adam Simon? Okay.

Buck: Okay? Julia Roberts, comes home, their daughter, the graduate.

Griffin: Yes, the new graduate.

BUCK: The new graduate.

GRIFFIN: The postgraduate.

(*The camera follows* JAN *as she goes to another window, and we see* BONNIE SHEROW, *a studio executive in her late twenties, cross the studio parking lot with* ADAM. *He pitches the same story to her.*)

ADAM: Griffin loved it. He just wanted me to run it by you. It's a hardy band of human survivors. Generations removed from the mother ship. They have no history, only mythology, they've lost all their technological knowledge, only rudimentary mathematical skills.

BONNIE (*overlapping*): Listen, why don't you write this down for me. Okay? I can't process it. Can you write it down for me, all right!

ADAM: It's not about words, it's about pictures. You've got to visualize it.

(*The camera follows them till we hear an offscreen crash.* BONNIE *and* ADAM *run across the bungalow yard to find a mail-room golf cart has run into Jimmy's bicycle.* JIMMY *lies on his back. Mail covers the ground.*)

BONNIE: Jimmy? Jimmy, are you okay? What happened? Are you all right?

CART DRIVER: Hey, kid.

JIMMY: In twenty-five words or less? I'd say my name is Jimmy Chase.

CART DRIVER: He came out of nowhere, ran right into me.

JIMMY: Hey, that's Adam Simon!

ADAM: How the hell you doing, kid, I was just at a meeting. I was just telling about it . . . Yeah, it was good.

(*The camera zooms in on a bundle of mail on the ground and focuses on a postcard. On the front we can read in black pen:* "You're Dead." *No one sees this. As the mail is picked up,* JOEL LEVISON, *the studio president, arrives.* SANDY *chases his car toward the bungalows.*

The camera pans to see REGGIE GOLDMAN, *pull up in a Porsche.* REGGIE, *midtwenties, leans out of his car to flirt with* JENNIFER NASH, *an actress in a red dress.*)

REGGIE: Rebecca DeMornay. Actually you're much better looking.

JENNIFER: Hmm, no. I'm not Rebecca DeMornay

REGGIE: Dead ringer.

JENNIFER: Thank you. Thank you very much.

REGGIE: Say, do you know where Joel Levison's office is?

JENNIFER: *The* Mr. Levison? Head of the studio?

(*A* TOUR GUIDE *strolls by with a group of Japanese tourists.*)

TOUR GUIDE: . . . And it will ruin the ending for you guys. But it's quite moving, it will rip your heart out. In fact, this is the area right here where we make a lot of decisions to give a green light to a picture like that. Right here. We're going to go about seventeen stories high if we can. We're going to continue to use all the Sony products. *Domo-arigato* to the Sony products, really. In fact if you need someone to eat some sashimi with you, give me a ring, because—

(LEVINSON *parks in front of his office.* SANDY *catches up to him as* CELIA *comes out to greet them.*)

LEVISON: The traffic from Malibu was just impossible.

CELIA: Morning, Joel.

LEVISON: Sandy, park the car, please. Morning Marty, Annie, Frank. (*To* CELIA:) What are the Japs doing here?

(CELIA *and* LEVISON *go into the office as* MARTY, ANNIE, *and* FRANK, *three studio executives, leave and walk across the bungalow court-yard.*)

ANNIE: So what's all the talk around here about "heads will roll"?

FRANK: The bank's putting the screws to us. Harvey Gold-man's son is coming out from Boston. I don't like it.

ANNIE: Reggie Goldman's a pipsqueak. Can't be serious.

MARTY: Some changes are going on here. It's always that way. Happened at Paramount two years ago; Columbia's going through it now. I hear we're looking to replace Griffin.

ANNIE: Griffin!

MARTY: Hmm-hmmm.

ANNIE: I don't believe it. With who?

MARTY: Berg or Kirkpatrick, maybe Larry Levy.

(*They pass Griffin's window, and we stay there. We see* JOAN TEWKES-

BURY *and* PAT RESNICK *in the middle of a story pitch.* GRIFFIN *interrupts them to answer the phone.*)

GRIFFIN: Yeah, well, I want to know why the security is so lax, that's why. I'll talk to you about it later. I'm in the middle of a pitch. Okay. (*To* PAT *and* JOAN:) Listen, go ahead.

PAT: Yeah okay. It's a TV star—

JOAN: Like a Donna Mills, a Joan Collins . . .

PAT: And she goes on safari to—

GRIFFIN: You're talking about a TV star in a motion picture?

PAT: Not a real TV star, it would be played by a movie star . . .

JOAN: A star star. Julia Roberts would be good, Dolly Parton would be good—

PAT: . . . Goldie, Julia, Michelle . . .

GRIFFIN: A movie star playing a TV star—

PAT: Bette, Lily, Dolly . . .

GRIFFIN: You know I like Goldie—

PAT: Goldie? Great! We have a relationship, and that would be great—

JOAN: Okay . . . Goldie goes to Africa, Goldie goes to Africa—

GRIFFIN: Goldie goes to Africa—

PAT: Goldie goes to Africa—

JOAN: And she becomes worshiped—

PAT: Well, she's found by this tribe—

GRIFFIN: Yes.

JOAN: Small, of small people, but then she has to go back to her life—

PAT: She's found by this tribe, and they worship her, but then—

GRIFFIN: Oh, I see, it's kind of a *Gods Must Be Crazy,* except the Coke bottle's now a television actress—

PAT: Yeah, exactly right. It's *Out of Africa* meets *Pretty Woman*—

JOAN: Well, but you know what—

PAT: And she has to decide whether to stay with the TV show or save this entire African tribe—

JOAN: It could be, it could be a man.

(ALAN RUDOLPH *walks past the bungalow. He sees* JIMMY.)

ALAN: Hey, where is Griffin Mill's office?

JIMMY: Right here. Hey! You're Martin Scorsese!

ALAN: No, but I know Harvey Keitel.

JIMMY: Hey, I know you do. Hey, I loved *Cape Fear.*

(WALTER and BUCK *pass. We follow them.*)

WALTER: My old man worked for Hitchcock. *Rope* was a masterpiece. The story wasn't any good, but he shot it without cuts, I hate all this cut . . . cut . . . cut . . .

BUCK: Oh yeah, well, what about Bertolucci's in that great tracking shot with Winger in *Sheltering Sky?*

WALTER: Didn't see it. *Touch of Evil,* that's the one. Welles, Hitchcock . . .

(*They pass* BONNIE *and her assistant,* WHITNEY GERSH. *We follow them.*)

WHITNEY: I've been here since eight o'clock, Bonnie. Honest, I was.

BONNIE: . . . In the commissary . . . I stuck my neck out to get you this job, who were you with?

WHITNEY: Err, with umm . . . Alan Rudolph.

BONNIE: What were you doing with Alan Rudolph?

WHITNEY: Well, no, he asked me to have coffee, and he was telling me this idea he had.

BONNIE: You're my assistant, you don't get involved with writers.

WHITNEY: But I wasn't getting involved. I was just listening to this amazing idea. I told him he could give it to you.

(*They bring us back to Griffin's window where* GRIFFIN *listens to* ALAN.)

GRIFFIN: What's your pitch?

ALAN: Well, does political scare you?

GRIFFIN: Political doesn't scare me. Radical political scares me, political political scares me.

ALAN: This is politely politically radical, but it's—

GRIFFIN: Is it funny?

ALAN: It's funny. It's fun—

GRIFFIN: It's a funny political thing.

ALAN: It's a funny—and it's a thriller too.

GRIFFIN: And it's a thriller too.

ALAN: And it's all at once.

GRIFFIN: So, uhh, what's the story?

ALAN: Well, I want Bruce Willis.

GRIFFIN: Um-huh.

ALAN: I think I can talk to him. It's a story about a senator, a bad guy senator at first. And he's traveling around the country on the country's dime, you know like that Sununu guy used to.

GRIFFIN: I see, so there's sort of a cynical political thriller comedy—

ALAN: Yeah, but it's got a heart in the right spot. And anyway, he has an accident.

GRIFFIN: An accident?

ALAN: Yeah, and he becomes clairvoyant, like a psychic.

GRIFFIN: Oh, I see.

ALAN: Yeah.

GRIFFIN: So it's kind of a psychic political thriller comedy with a heart.

(JAN *enters and gives* GRIFFIN *his mail. On top is the postcard seen after Jimmy's accident.*)

ALAN: With a heart. Not unlike *Ghost* meets *The Manchurian Candidate.*

GRIFFIN: Go on, go on, I'm listening.

ALAN: Anyway, he can start to read people's minds, and when he gets to the president's mind, it's completely blank. Completely blank.

(GRIFFIN *reads the postcard. It says:* "I HATE YOUR GUTS ASSHOLE.")

JAN: Can I get you anything?

ALAN: I'd like a beer.

JAN: We don't have beer.

ALAN: Wine, red wine, please. Of course, someone gets killed at the end. They always do in political thrillers.

* * *

INTERIOR: GRIFFIN'S OUTER OFFICE. DAY. LATER.
Phone rings. JAN *answers.* GRIFFIN *comes out of his office with* JIM, *another writer. Simultaneous conversations occur between* JAN *and a caller* (POSTCARD WRITER) *and between* JIM *and* GRIFFIN.

JAN: Griffin Mill's office.

POSTCARD WRITER: Yeah, I know that, can you put him on?

GRIFFIN: It's an intriguing idea, Jim. Let it sit with me a few days.

JAN: May I ask who's calling, please?

POSTCARD WRITER: I'd like to speak to Griffin Mill.

JIM: And we've got to get someone really dangerous.

JAN: He's in a meeting right now. Give me your number, and I'll have him get back to you.

GRIFFIN: I'm with you there.

JIM: You know, Bruce Willis or Mel Gibson.

POSTCARD WRITER: He'll get back to me? Shit.

GRIFFIN: Great. Let me get back to you.

JIM: Thanks.

JAN: Excuse me, sir?

POSTCARD WRITER: Shit. He'll get back to me?

(JIM *leaves.* GRIFFIN *turns his attention to* JAN.)

GRIFFIN: Have you seen my Binaca anywhere?

POSTCARD WRITER: Do you know how many times I've heard that?

JAN: Who is this?

POSTCARD WRITER: If you don't get back to me, tell him—
(*The* POSTCARD WRITER *hangs up.*
BONNIE *enters office.*)

BONNIE: Griffin? I read that script . . . It's a nice idea.

GRIFFIN (*to* JAN): Who is that?

JAN: I don't know, he didn't say.

GRIFFIN: What do you mean, he didn't say?

BONNIE: . . . I don't know how you are going to cast it though. The lead character is a fifty-year-old female circus performer, a fire-eater.

GRIFFIN: Let me read the coverage.

BONNIE: Listen, are we still having lunch with Aaron Cant and his people?

GRIFFIN: Yeah. What time?

BONNIE: I made it for one o'clock.

(GRIFFIN *goes into his inner office.*)

BONNIE (*to* JAN): Bad day?

JAN: He's having writer's block. Griffin, you have a meeting with Hotter and Frank Saus this afternoon.

GRIFFIN: What time?

JAN: At three o'clock.

GRIFFIN: I'll be here. Put this morning's meeting in the computer.

JAN: All right.

GRIFFIN: Thanks.

BONNIE: Are you going out? I'll go with you.

GRIFFIN: No, I'm going to see Levison. I'll meet you there. Order me a Caesar salad and a Crystal Geyser. Thanks.

INTERIOR: LEVISON'S OFFICE. DAY.

GRIFFIN *walks into the reception area where* JIMMY *drops off more mail. Then he walks into the main office where he finds* LEVISON, REGGIE, *and* WALTER. REGGIE *picks through a stack of starlets' head-shots.* GRIFFIN *starts to walk into the inner office.* CELIA *tries to stop him.*

JIMMY: Okay, I'm on five? Thanks, Sandy.

CELIA: Griffin, you can't go in there. He's in a meeting.

LEVISON: It's all right, Celia. Griffin, I don't think you've met Reg Goldman. You know his father, Harvey.

GRIFFIN: Yes, of course. Hi—hi, Reg, from the bank in Boston.

LEVISON: Reg is out here for a couple of weeks.

GRIFFIN: Great. Business or pleasure?

REGGIE: A little of both, I hope.

LEVISON: Reg is thinking of getting into production, Griffin.

GRIFFIN: Oh really.

REGGIE: Yeah, beats work, doesn't it, Griff? I'd like to play some tennis though, you play tennis?

GRIFFIN: Tennis? No, no, no, I'm too busy.

REGGIE: I was just asking Walter here do you know Meg Ryan? Do you know if she's seeing somebody?

GRIFFIN: Umm, yeah, Reg, she's married.

REGGIE: Shit. What about Winona Ryder?

GRIFFIN: Um, well, uhh, you know, actually Walter is the guy to talk to. Walter's got everybody's number.

LEVISON: Was there anything?

GRIFFIN: Uhh, no, you're real busy.

REGGIE: I want that number, goddamn it, I want that number.

CELIA: Oh boy.

(REGGIE *holds up another headshot.*)

REGGIE: What about this one here, she done anything?

(*Cut to:*)

INTERIOR: LEVISON'S OFFICE. OUTER FOYER.

GRIFFIN *approaches* CELIA.

GRIFFIN: Celia . . .

CELIA: Griffin. Don't ask.

GRIFFIN: Don't ask, you don't know or don't ask, I don't want to know.

CELIA: Just don't ask. Look, if it's Reggie Goldman you're concerned about, forget it. But be nice to him. He represents a lot of money for this company—

GRIFFIN: It's not Reggie I'm worried about; it's Larry Levy.

CELIA: Larry Levy? Larry Levy's at Fox, isn't he?

GRIFFIN: Ohhuhh. Come on, Celia . . . Should I be looking for a job?

(*A call comes in.* CELIA *picks up, cutting off* GRIFFIN.)

CELIA: Joel Levison's office. Oh, Brad, yeah. What? No, we couldn't sign Anjelica Huston for that project. She's booked for the next two years.

(*Cut to:*)

* * *

INTERIOR: LE RESTAURANT. DAY.

ANJELICA HUSTON, JOHN CUSAK, *and* LARRY LEVY *are seated at lunch.*

>ANJELICA HUSTON: It's a ghost story, but it's not *Ghost.*

>JOHN CUSAK: We call it *Unnaturized;* it's a supernatural thing.

(GRIFFIN *enters the foyer. He runs into the actor* JOEL GREY, *who is leaving.*)

>GRIFFIN: Joel, Griffin Mill.

>JOEL GREY: You're Griffin Mill? No, no, no . . .

>GRIFFIN: Yeah.

>JOEL GREY: Really?

>GRIFFIN: Good to see you. I'm a big fan of yours.

>JOEL GREY: I have that tie.

>GRIFFIN: You do?

(JOEL GREY *is gone. The hostess shows* GRIFFIN *to the table where* BONNIE *is already seated with other studio executives.*)

>GRIFFIN: Did you order for me?

>BONNIE: Yeah.

(*Everyone greets* GRIFFIN.)

>GRIFFIN: Hi, everybody. (*To* BONNIE:) Lunching with the enemy?

(*Everyone groans.*)

>ELLEN: Oh, come on. So what's this we hear about Larry Levy?

>GRIFFIN: Larry Levy? If he had half a brain, he'd be dangerous.

>BONNIE: Aaron says he's coming to the studio.

(LEVY *looks over from his lunch. He knows something* GRIFFIN *doesn't.*)

>GRIFFIN: Aaron says? Why would you believe anything he says?

>BONNIE: What? He's over there.

>GRIFFIN: Who? Levy?

(GRIFFIN *sees* LEVY.)

>BONNIE: With Anjelica Huston and John Cusak.

GRIFFIN: He's in over his head. He's going to drown over there.

ELLEN: He's quite the golden boy at Fox these days. Did you see that piece in *Variety* last week?

(GRIFFIN *gets up to greet* ANJELICA HUSTON *and* JOHN CUSAK *as they leave.*)

GRIFFIN: Anjelica, Griffin Mill.

ANJELICA HUSTON: Oh, hi.

GRIFFIN: Good to see you. You're looking great. Hey, Johnny—Griffin Mill, big fan of yours.

JOHN CUSAK: Yeah.

GRIFFIN: Going to be at Telluride this year?

JOHN CUSAK: Uh, no, Park City.

GRIFFIN: Uh, great. See you there.

JOHN CUSAK: Okay.

(JOHN CUSAK *and* ANJELICA HUSTON *are gone.*)

ELLEN: So what's happening with *Glass Box?*

GRIFFIN: Could we please talk about something other than Hollywood for a change? We're educated people.

EVERYONE: Sure. Okay. Fine, Griffin. (*Etc.*)

(*Pause. No one says a word. They look around uncomfortably at each other.*

A pause, then everyone laughs.

Cut to:)

EXTERIOR: LE RESTAURANT. DAY.

GRIFFIN *loads* JAN *into a sportscar with* AARON.

GRIFFIN: Call you later.

(GRIFFIN *goes to his car, pays the valet. He gets in. From inside the car, he can read the postcard stuck under his windshield:* "WE HAD A MEETING. I TOLD YOU MY IDEA. YOU SAID YOU'D GET BACK TO ME. WELL?" *He turns on the wiper, brings the card over to his side, and reaches out the window to pluck it off. He turns it over. Bogart with a gun. He tucks it into his jacket.*)

*   *   *

INTERIOR: GRIFFIN'S INNER OFFICE. LATER.

GRIFFIN *opens a drawer and adds Bogart card to a pile of postcards. They all have cryptic messages on them:* "YOU SAID YOU'D GET BACK TO ME"; "IS IT YOU OR ME?"; "I'M WAITING FOR YOUR CALL"; "I'M LOSING MY PATIENCE"; "NOW YOU'VE MADE ME ANGRY"; *etc.* JAN *is updating him on his messages.*

JAN: Shouldn't you talk to somebody about this?

GRIFFIN: What?

JAN: These postcards. You've gotten five in two weeks.

GRIFFIN: Seven, actually.

JAN: Griffin, why don't you just talk to studio security?

GRIFFIN: Why? I'm supposed to call Walter Stuckel and say what? (*Acting it out.*) "Walter, listen. Someone is sending me poison-pen letters, and I would like for you to make me the object of more ridicule and abuse, now that things are already shaky for me here." No, I don't think so, Jan.

JAN: I think they're coming from a writer.

GRIFFIN: A writer? Which one?

JAN: Take your pick.

(*She hangs there.*)

GRIFFIN: Is there anything else?

JAN: Yes. Your attorney phoned. He wants you to come to a party at his house tonight.

GRIFFIN: Get me out of it. Tell him I've got to go to a screening.

JAN: No, not that attorney. Dick Mellen.

GRIFFIN: Oh. Dick. What time?

JAN: Seven-thirty cocktails, dinner at eight, bring a date.

BONNIE (*offscreen*): If I have to read one more goddamn sensitive male-bonding script . . .

(BONNIE *slides by* JAN *into Griffin's office, carrying a script. She collapses into his arms.*)

JAN: Oh, and Bonnie Sherow's here to see you.

GRIFFIN: Ask her to come in. Oh, there she is.

(JAN *leaves.*)

BONNIE: Griffin, could we go to the Springs this weekend?
I want to have a massage, I want to have a long soak in
a hot mineral tub, and I want to have margaritas adminis-
tered intravenously.

GRIFFIN: I have a party tonight at Dick Mellen's. You want
to come?

BONNIE: Oh, God! Movie stars and power players.

GRIFFIN: And vodka.

BONNIE: Sure.

GRIFFIN: It's an early dinner. We'll make an appearance
and go back to my place.

BONNIE: Can we?

GRIFFIN: Yeah.

(*Cut to:*)

EXTERIOR/INTERIOR. DICK MELLEN'S HOUSE. NIGHT.

The house is a bad developer's idea of postmodern. JACK LEMMON *is
playing the piano.* DICK MELLEN *chats with* HARRY BELAFONTE.
GRIFFIN *and* BONNIE *enter the house. They say hello to* MARLEE MATLIN
and her interpreter.

GRIFFIN: How are ya? Marlee, this is Bonnie Sherow. She
read *Tales of Fury.*

BONNIE: I loved it. It was wonderful! And I think you are
perfect for Ariel . . . perfect for the part . . . We're gonna
make just a couple changes in the third act.

GRIFFIN: You should set up a meeting.

(MELLEN, *Griffin's lawyer, goes to them.*)

GRIFFIN (*to* BONNIE): You don't talk script changes at
parties.

BONNIE: All right, I'm sorry.

MELLEN (*reaching them*): Don't you look beautiful.

(*He can't remember Bonnie's name.*)

GRIFFIN: You know Bonnie Sherow.

MELLEN: How are you, dear? You're at Tri Star, right?

BONNIE: No, I'm . . .

GRIFFIN: She's at the studio.

MELLEN: Yeah, that's what I meant. (*He turns to the waiter:*) Bring Mr. Mill a martini. And Bunny, how 'bout you?

GRIFFIN: No, actually I'll have a mimosa.

BONNIE: I'll have a martini.

MELLEN: Rod Steiger's here. Why don't you talk to him about that Rudolph project. He's not hot about it, but maybe he'll at least read it for you. (*He sees* HARRY BELAFONTE.) Do you know Harry Belafonte? He's in town for a couple of days. (*He calls:*) Harry?

(HARRY BELAFONTE *comes up.* MELLEN *introduces them.* BONNIE *engulfs* BELAFONTE *in praise and manages to pull him away.* MELLEN *walks with* GRIFFIN.)

BONNIE: Harry Belafonte? Swoon. I'm a big fan of yours. I saw you accept the Nelson Mandela Courage Award . . .

(*She exits.*)

GRIFFIN: Ah, I got some . . .

MELLEN: Some what?

GRIFFIN: I've been getting some funny postcards. You know, harassment kind of stuff.

MELLEN: No, I don't know. Tell me. What are you talking about?

GRIFFIN: Some writer I must have brushed off (*pauses as* MELLEN *greets guests*) keeps sending these postcards . . . faxes.

MELLEN: Not threats? You talking about threats?

GRIFFIN: No. Yes. I don't know. But he's pissed off.

MELLEN: I thought writers were your long suit. You're the writers' exec, aren't you? That's your rep. Sure it isn't some actress you brushed off?

(BONNIE *spots* LEVY *entering with* SALLY KELLERMAN. *They talk to* JEFF GOLDBLUM. *She walks by* GRIFFIN *and nudges him.*)

BONNIE: Levy's here.

(*She keeps moving.*)

GRIFFIN: Dick, Dick, what's he doing here?

MELLEN: Goldblum? He's a friend.

GRIFFIN: No, Larry Levy.

MELLEN: Levy? He came with Sally. He's a buddy.

GRIFFIN: No, what's going on with my job? I run into Levy everywhere I look. He's in my face.

MELLEN: Larry Levy's a comer. That's what comers do. They get in your face. You're a comer too. You can handle him. Stop worrying about him.

GRIFFIN: So the rumors are true.

MELLEN: The rumors are always true. You know that.

GRIFFIN: I'm always the last to hear about them.

MELLEN: You're the last one to believe. I told you that.

GRIFFIN: Am I out?

MELLEN: Not out. But you better start thinking about a roommate. Relax, you can handle it. Make him work for you. (*Goes to* LARRY:) Larry!

LEVY: Dick, sorry to crash your party.

(GRIFFIN *and* BONNIE *retire to the other end of the pool.* MELLEN *walks past* REGGIE, *who is with* KATHEY IRELAND, *a model.*)

REGGIE: Great party, Dick.

MELLEN: Good, did you get some food?

REGGIE: Not yet.

INTERIOR: GRIFFIN'S HOT TUB. NIGHT.

BONNIE *reads a script in the hot tub.* GRIFFIN *edits a guest list for the Museum Gala.*

BONNIE: Listen to this: "He lifts her dress. She kisses him harder. He puts his hands in her underpants. She grabs his shoulders. He pulls her dress above her waist. He rubs against her wide, soft belly. Slowly he pushes her panties down to her knees. She is faint with passion. She arches her back, and he lowers her down onto the buckboard. The horses snort and whinny; they, too, seem to be feeling her passion. The camera moves in on the nostrils of the horse as the buckboard begins to shake." (*She drops the script on the water.*) Can you believe it? Steve recommended that script. He says they're really hot for it over at Universal. They're gonna have a bidding war.

(GRIFFIN *is not paying attention; he's lost in his own thoughts.*)

GRIFFIN: I heard a pitch today. It wasn't bad, but I'm stuck on a story point, though.

BONNIE: I'm the story editor. Go.

GRIFFIN: New York City. Madison Avenue. Big advertising agency. An account executive makes a presentation to someone he wants as a client, and the client promises to get back to him.

BONNIE: Does it have to be advertising?

GRIFFIN: That's not the problem. The account executive keeps waiting for the client to call him back, to tell him what he thought of the idea, to tell him if he got the job, but the client never calls. The account executive gets so . . . pissed off . . . so frustrated, that he becomes obsessed, so he decides to drive the client crazy.

BONNIE: What does he do?

GRIFFIN: Sends him threatening postcards. It's not important. Here's the problem. How long do you think the account executive harasses the client before he becomes dangerous?

BONNIE: Does it have to be advertising?

GRIFFIN: How long?

BONNIE: Well, if it were me . . .

GRIFFIN: A month?

BONNIE: Three months. No. More. Five months. To be dangerous, five months.

GRIFFIN: That's what I said. About five months.

BONNIE: Who's the writer?

GRIFFIN: I don't know.

BONNIE: You don't know the writer who pitched you the idea?

GRIFFIN (*recovers*): A couple of kids. A team. TV writers.

BONNIE (*not interested*): Oh. (*She warms up.*) Can we go to bed now? I'm starting to wrinkle.

(BONNIE *rolls over and starts to make love to* GRIFFIN.)

* * *

EXTERIOR/INTERIOR: GEOFFERY'S RESTAURANT. DAY.

LEVY *is just finishing breakfast with* LEVISON. *They shake hands, and* LEVY *leaves passing* BURT REYNOLDS *and* CHARLES CHAMPLIN, *the film critic.*

LEVY: Burt? Larry Levy. I hope you don't remember me, and if you do, I hope there are no hard feelings. I was only working for Kastner at the time.

BURT REYNOLDS: Who's that?

CHARLES CHAMPLIN: An exec over at Fox. Or he was until this breakfast, anyway.

(GRIFFIN *pulls into the parking lot. As he gets out of his car, he sees* LEVY *get into his Mercedes. They eye each other.* GRIFFIN *enters the restaurant. Inside he walks past tables filled with film executives and celebrities.*)

HOSTESS: Good morning, Mr. Mill. Welcome to Geoffrey's.

GRIFFIN (*walking past hostess*): Hi, Susan, how are you? I'm with Joel. (*Walking past* BURT REYNOLDS.) Hi, Burt, Griffin Mill. Hi, Charles. (*Shakes hands, walks past.*)

BURT REYNOLDS: Asshole.

CHARLES CHAMPLIN: One of a breed.

BURT REYNOLDS: Actually, not one of a breed. There's a whole breed of them. They're breeding them.

(*He continues to* LEVISON'S *table and sits down.* LEVISON *is eating.* LEVY *was obviously there, and his place has not yet been cleared away.*)

GRIFFIN: So, Joel, you're losing your touch. You schedule these meetings so close together, that last guy didn't have time to finish his breakfast.

LEVISON: He'd already eaten. He gets up early. You went to Mellen's last night, I hear?

(*A busboy comes by the table.*)

GRIFFIN: Will you take this away, please. (*To* LEVISON:) Yes, I did.

LEVISON: How is he?

GRIFFIN: He's fine. (*To busboy:*) Vittel, please.

LEVISON: You left early. Why?

GRIFFIN: We had to work on the museum party.

(*Pause. He knows what's going on.*)

GRIFFIN: I will not work for Larry Levy.

LEVISON: I'm not asking you to . . .

GRIFFIN: I report to you. If I have to report to Levy, I quit.

LEVISON: You can't quit. I won't let you quit. You have a year and a half on your contract, and I will sue you for breach if you do not show up in the office every day, with a smile.

GRIFFIN: Why Levy?

LEVISON: Levy was available. He's good on material. You're good with writers. We're a team. He's a new member of the team. That's all. He can make us all look good.

GRIFFIN (*to waiter*): This is a red-wine glass. Can I have my water in a water glass, please?

LEVISON: Well?

GRIFFIN: I'll have to think about it, Joel.

LEVISON: I want an answer this afternoon.

GRIFFIN: Well, I have to go out to Palmdale. The director on *The Lonely Room* set is giving Lily a hard time. I'll be back around five.

LEVISON: So call after five.

GRIFFIN: I'll get back to you.

(GRIFFIN *looks at the nearly full fruit plate and half-eaten bran muffin* LEVY *has left. He leaves. As he passes* BURT REYNOLDS:)

BURT REYNOLDS (*to* CHARLES CHAMPLIN): He's still hanging on.

INTERIOR: GRIFFIN'S OUTER/INNER OFFICE. DAY.

It is late afternoon. GRIFFIN *goes into his office and looks at his mail. There is an accordion postcard, folded and taped, among the letters. He picks it up and opens it.*

JAN (*on intercom*): Griffin? Joel Levison on line two.

GRIFFIN: No, no, I'll get back to him.

(*The pictures dangle in front of him. He reads the message:* "GRIFFIN MILL—IN THE NAME OF ALL WRITERS—I'M GOING TO KILL YOU." *There is no postmark on the card.*)

JAN: You want me to tell Joel Levison you'll get back to him?

GRIFFIN: Yeah. I don't want to hear what he's got to say.

(*Cut to:*)

INTERIOR: JAN'S OFFICE. DAY.

GRIFFIN *is at Jan's desk showing her the postcard.*

GRIFFIN: How'd this get here?

JAN: The mail.

GRIFFIN: But this doesn't have a postmark. This was delivered by hand . . .

JAN: Not to me. It came with the mail.

(*She calls to* JIMMY, *who is in another office reading something on a desk:*)

JAN: Jimmy!

(JIMMY *approaches.*)

JIMMY: Hey.

GRIFFIN: Do you know anything about this? Who delivered it? Where it came from?

JIMMY (*ponders*): Umm, mail room?

GRIFFIN: I want to know how it got to the goddamn mail room. Would you find out for me and get back to me, please?

(JIMMY *starts to leave as* GRIFFIN *turns to* JAN.)

GRIFFIN: You go with him.

JAN: You want ME to go to the mail room?

GRIFFIN: Yes, I want you to go to the mail room, and while you're there, I want ONE copy of the rewrites of *The Lonely Room* in white pages. No color. And find out how this got in my mail.

JAN: Yes, sir. You'll get your own phones, I take it?

GRIFFIN: Yes, Jan. I'll get my own phones.

(*They leave, and* GRIFFIN *starts going through the appointment book* JAN *keeps for him. He mutters as he goes back through the weeks.*)

GRIFFIN: Son of a bitch. Five months. One, two, three, four, five. Calls unreturned . . .

(*The calendar is dense with names, canceled meetings, travel plans, breakfast-to-dinner appointments, screenings. He goes down the phone log. He looks down the* TIME RETURNED *column. A few blanks. He turns the calendar and the phone log ahead another month, and finds a week with ten unreturned calls.* DAVID KAHANE. *He turns to the next week. Five unreturned calls.* DAVID KAHANE. *The next week. Two calls.* DAVID KAHANE. *He is now on the computer.*)

GRIFFIN: Come on. Kahane, Kahane.

(*He takes a* Writer's Guild Directory *from a shelf next to the desk and matches names. He checks Kahane's name in the guild directory. He's there. Under credits: a blank space.*)

GRIFFIN: *H-J-K.* Kahane. Unproduced. Gotcha!

(*For the first time in months,* GRIFFIN *is in control.*)

EXTERIOR: JUNE'S HOUSE. NIGHT.

Griffin's Range Rover comes to a stop in front of a pleasant house in Westwood with a large picture window. The room inside is well lit, and it appears to be an artist's studio. All the paintings are icy and cold abstractions. He sees the artist, JUNE GUDMUNDSDOTTIR, *working on her paintings. This is not what he expected.* GRIFFIN *checks the phone number and dials it from his mobile phone. Suddenly, there are strange flashes of light from inside the house. The phone rings many times before* JUNE *seems to hear it.* GRIFFIN *gets out of his car and approaches the house with his phone in hand. He moves right up to the front window and watches her. He can hear the phone ringing, both inside the house and on his phone. She pays no attention. She takes Polaroid pictures of herself. She finally hears the phone, uncovers it from the art supplies in the room, and answers it. This takes her out of Griffin's view, and he moves into a patio area and now sees her from a side window. He approaches the window until he is very close.*

JUNE: Hello?

GRIFFIN: Yes, hello. Is David Kahane there, please?

(JUNE *puts the phone to her chest and calls.*)

JUNE: David? Dave? (*She looks at her work, waiting for him to answer, then realizes he is not there.*) Hello, I'm really sorry, I forgot. He's gone out.

GRIFFIN: Oh, I see.

JUNE: Who's this?

GRIFFIN: Griffin Mill.

JUNE: Oh, the dead man.

GRIFFIN: What did you say?

JUNE: Oh, nothing.

GRIFFIN: About me being a dead man?

JUNE: Just a nickname David has for you.

GRIFFIN: Oh, I see. That's a funny nickname. So, I suppose your husband doesn't like me very much.

(JUNE *has moved so* GRIFFIN *has to move to another window to see her.*)

JUNE: I don't have a husband.

GRIFFIN: Well, I suppose David doesn't like me very much.

JUNE: David's gone to the cinema.

GRIFFIN: When will he be back?

JUNE: When the film's over, I presume.

GRIFFIN: And you are?

JUNE: June.

GRIFFIN: June . . . ?

JUNE: Oh, here we go. You want to know my last name? You won't be able to pronounce it. No one can.

GRIFFIN: Try me.

JUNE: Gudmundsdottir.

GRIFFIN: Gudmundsdottir.

JUNE: Gudmundsdottir.

GRIFFIN: Gudmundsdottir. How's that?

JUNE: Hey. Very good.

GRIFFIN: Thanks. What do people usually say?

JUNE: Oh, don't ask. Anything from "good dog's water" to "goulash water."

GRIFFIN: Are you English?

JUNE: Yes. No. Not really.

GRIFFIN: Where are you kinda sorta not from?

JUNE: Do you want the long story or the short one?

GRIFFIN: The long one.

JUNE: No, you'd never believe it. The short one is "Iceland."

GRIFFIN: Iceland. I didn't know anybody came from Iceland. I thought it was just a block of ice.

JUNE: It's very green, actually.

GRIFFIN: Really? I thought that was Greenland.

JUNE: No, Greenland's very icy. Iceland's very green. They switched names to fool the Vikings who tried to steal their women.

GRIFFIN: Oh, I see (*pronounced like* icy).

JUNE: No, Blue sea . . .

GRIFFIN: Red sea.

JUNE: No, no, no. No red.

GRIFFIN: You're a painter.

JUNE: How did you guess?

GRIFFIN: What movie did David go to?

JUNE: He went to the Rialto in Pasadena. He always goes there.

GRIFFIN: What's showing?

JUNE: *Bicycle Thief,* I think.

GRIFFIN: It's a good movie. Have you seen it?

JUNE: I don't go to the movies.

GRIFFIN: You don't? Why not?

JUNE: Ohh. Life's too short. I have to hang up now.

(*She hangs up.*)

INTERIOR: THEATER. NIGHT.

GRIFFIN *enters the dark auditorium. A person sitting in the back row withdraws his boots from the aisle just in time to prevent* GRIFFIN *from tripping on them.* GRIFFIN *sits.*

The Bicycle Thief.

As the final scene plays, Griffin *looks around the theater.*
The lights come up. Griffin *is in a middle row, a few seats in from the*
aisle. The audience consists of a small crowd of slightly depressed
film lovers, dressed in dark clothes, ten people in all. Griffin *studies*
them: an older couple, a few women including Mrs. Bunny; *couples*
together. And here comes a single White Man, *the right age.* Griffin
follows him into the lobby, tentatively.

> Griffin: David Kahane?
>
> White Man: No, you have the wrong guy, man.

(*He passes. And then behind him we see* David Kahane, *thirty-two,*
wire-framed glasses, dark hair. Griffin *spots him and goes to him.*)

> Griffin: David Kahane? Griffin Mill.
>
> Kahane: Griffin Mill . . . yeah!?
>
> Griffin: Great movie, huh? It's so refreshing to see some-
> thing like this after all the cop movies and things we do.
> Maybe we'll do a remake.
>
> Kahane: You'd probably give it a happy ending.
>
> Griffin: No, no. We'd keep it pure.
>
> Kahane: Pure. Right.
>
> Griffin: You want to write it?
>
> Kahane: Don't fuck with me, Mill.

(Mrs. Bunny *passes between them on her way out.*)

> Griffin: I'm not fucking with you. I said I'd get back to
> you, didn't I?
>
> Kahane: Yeah, six months ago. I thought you'd forgotten.
>
> Griffin: You were angry.
>
> Kahane: Maybe.
>
> Griffin: Do you want to talk about it?
>
> Kahane (*stops, studies* Griffin): Okay. Sure.
>
> Griffin: Great. Let's let the studio buy us a drink.
>
> Kahane: Well, if you don't mind a place where you don't
> have any suck with the maître d', I know a bar down the
> street.
>
> Griffin: Let's go.

(*They leave.*)

* * *

INTERIOR: KARAOKE BAR. NIGHT.

GRIFFIN *and* KAHANE *are at a table. There are Asian men in suits, a slew of hostesses, and a karaoke machine. A drunk Japanese man holds a microphone and sings.*

KAHANE: You ever been to Japan?

GRIFFIN: Yeah, once, on a location scout with Steven . . . Spielberg.

KAHANE: I lived there for a year. Student year abroad.

GRIFFIN: Great. I wish, I wish I'd done that.

KAHANE: I think about it a lot. I'll never forget it.

GRIFFIN: You should write about it.

KAHANE: I did. Don't you remember?

GRIFFIN: What?

(*The drinks arrive.*)

KAHANE: *Aregato.* My idea. About an American student who goes to Japan. That was my pitch. The one you were supposed to get back to me on.

(GRIFFIN *is confused.*)

KAHANE: You don't remember, do you?

(*The song is over.* GRIFFIN *applauds briefly.*)

GRIFFIN: Of course, I remember.

KAHANE: You never got back to me.

GRIFFIN: Listen, I was an asshole, all right? It comes with the job. I'm sorry. I really am. I know how angry it must have made you. I'll make it up to you, that's what I'm here for. I'm gonna give you a deal, David. I'm not going to guarantee I'll make the movie, but I'm gonna give you a shot. Let's just stop all the postcard shit, all right? I'm here to say that I would like to start over. Friends?

(GRIFFIN *offers his hand, but* KAHANE *doesn't shake.* KAHANE *watches him, and finally* GRIFFIN *puts his hand down without saying a word.*)

KAHANE: Fuck you, Mill. You're a liar.

GRIFFIN: You're stepping over the line, David.

KAHANE: You didn't come out here to see *The Bicycle Thief.* You came in five minutes before the picture ended. You nearly tripped over my feet. What'd you do, call my house? Speak to the ice queen? You'd like her, Mill. She's a lot like you. All heart. You're on my list, pal, and nothing's going to change that.

(KAHANE *gets up and walks.*)

KAHANE: See you in the next reel, asshole.

(KAHANE *leaves.*)

EXTERIOR: STREET. NIGHT.

GRIFFIN *leaves the bar. He walks past the theater and around the corner to his car and unlocks it. Just as he is about to get in,* KAHANE *speaks from the shadows.*

KAHANE: That's a nice boat you got there, Movie Exec. . . . It's me. The writer. Still wanna buy my story?

GRIFFIN: I told you . . . I'd give you a deal. Stop by the studio first thing in the morning, and we'll work something out.

KAHANE: And who'll I ask for? Larry Levy?

(GRIFFIN *starts to follow* KAHANE *down the sidewalk.*)

GRIFFIN: What's Larry Levy got to do with this? How do you know about Larry Levy?

KAHANE: Don't you read the trades? The *New York Times* Business Section? He's moving in . . . you're moving out. You can't make a deal, that's what they say. Yesterday's news.

GRIFFIN (*calling to him*): Wait a minute. Wait a minute.

(KAHANE *stops.*)

KAHANE: Can I borrow your mobile phone? Huh? (*He mocks taking a phone from him.*) Larry Levy? Yeah, David Kahane here. Listen, Larry, guess who's making promises about getting pictures made—to writers in parking lots. Guess what dumb son-of-a-bitch executive is trying to take advantage of me! Do you realize how unstoppable this guy is? You know I cannot wait to tell the world that when Griffin Mill can't cut the pressure at work, he drives out to Pasadena to pick fights with writers! (*He turns and walks toward his car, saying:*) Tell

Larry Levy to give me a call. You know, word is out that he's going to start making some meaningful pictures at the studio. For a change.

EXTERIOR: PARKING LOT. NIGHT.

GRIFFIN *follows* KAHANE *to his car.* KAHANE *unlocks the passenger door and puts his briefcase inside.*

GRIFFIN: Let's forget this. Just stop all the postcard shit.

KAHANE (*furious, pushing* GRIFFIN *back against a railing over a stairwell*): I don't write postcards! I write scripts!

GRIFFIN (*screaming back*): We're both wrong! Okay!

KAHANE: No, you're wrong, buddy! You're in over your head. That's why you're losing your job. And then what are you going to do? I can write, but what can you do?

(GRIFFIN *puts his hand on the door window and starts to close the door.*)

GRIFFIN: I said, Let's forget this.

(KAHANE *pushes the door toward him and sends him reeling over a broken railing and down a four-foot drop to the level below. It is a bad fall.* KAHANE *is immediately sobered. He jumps down to the lower level to help him.* GRIFFIN *pushes him away, and they struggle. Then* GRIFFIN *smashes him into a pond of trapped water. He grinds his face into the ground.*)

GRIFFIN: KEEP it to yourself, goddamn it. Keep it to yourself.

(GRIFFIN *leaves the unconscious* KAHANE *face down in the water and walks away. Several yards away, he stops and looks back.* KAHANE *doesn't move.* GRIFFIN *cautiously goes back. He looks at the inert body. He turns it over.* KAHANE *is dead.* GRIFFIN *turns* KAHANE *back over. He strips off his watch and billfold, and leaves him. He looks back at the car and sees his hand print on the car window. He goes to it, picks up a piece of broken railing, and smashes it. Then he walks away, unseen.*)

INTERIOR: LEVISON'S BUNGALOW. DAY.

BONNIE, LEVY, *and the rest of the team are having a meeting.*

LEVY: . . . Over three hundred million worldwide.

BONNIE: Larry, I don't believe you've met my assistant, Whitney Gersh.

LEVY: No, I haven't.

(*He shakes hands with her.*

REGGIE *sits on a phone behind them, going through a book of actresses.*)

INTERIOR: LEVISON'S INNER OFFICE. DAY.

LEVISON *talks to* WALTER *as* CELIA *enters. As she talks, Griffin's car drives by the outside window.*

CELIA: Excuse me, Walter. Joel, Griffin still isn't in. But I really think we have to start the meeting.

LEVISON: Okay, Celia, thank you.

WALTER: Remember a movie called *D.O.A.?*

LEVISON: Sure I do. Eddie O'Brien and Pam Griffin. Disney did a remake in '87 or '88.

WALTER: Well, I think we got pretty much the same situation.

LEVISON: Keep our noses clean, Walter—

(And LEVISON *is out and into the meeting room next door.*

GRIFFIN *enters.*)

GRIFFIN: Hello, and sorry I'm late.

CELIA: You certainly are . . .

(*Outside, we see* WALTER *approach* JAN.)

(LEVISON *returns.*)

LEVISON: Griffin, you missed the formal welcoming ceremony this morning. You know Larry Levy . . .

GRIFFIN: Of course. Hi, Larry.

LEVY: Hi, Griffin.

LEVISON: Larry was able to get out of Fox a week earlier than he thought, and has come aboard as of this morning.

GRIFFIN: Great. Let's start.

LEVISON: In fact, Larry was just in the middle of something here.

LEVY: No, no, I was just killing time waiting for Griffin.

LEVISON: No, finish. (*To* LEVY:) What were you saying?

LEVY: I was just saying that I have yet to meet a writer who could change water into wine. But there is a tendency to treat them that way.

LEVISON: Not at this studio.

LEVY: A million, a million and a half for these scripts. It's nuts. And, I think, avoidable. Let me ask you something. When was the last time any of you bought a ticket for a movie; that you actually paid your own money to see—

GRIFFIN: Last night, in Pasadena. *The Bicycle Thief.*

(GRIFFIN *realizes that he has just placed himself at the scene of Kahane's death in front of a room full of witnesses.*)

BONNIE: You? Went to see *The Bicycle Thief?*

WHITNEY: I love that film. It's a great film.

LEVY (*seizing control again*): It's an art movie. That doesn't count. I'm talking about movie movies.

(*He looks around the room. The team looks very uncomfortable.*)

LEVISON: Jesus, people.

LEVY: Look, all I'm just saying is that there's a lot of time and money to be saved if we come up with these stories on our own.

BONNIE: And where are these stories coming from, Larry?

LEVY: Anywhere, anywhere. It doesn't matter. Anywhere. Here, from the newspaper. Pick a story, any story.

(*He hands the newspaper to* STEVE REEVE.)

STEVE REEVE: Um . . . "Immigrants Protest Budget Cuts in Literacy Program."

LEVY: Human spirit overcoming economic adversity. Sounds like Horatio Alger in the barrio. You put in Jimmy Smits, you got a sexy *Stand and Deliver*. Next?

(*He hands the newspaper to* MARTY GROSSMAN, *vice-president of marketing.*)

MARTY: Larry, this really isn't my field.

LEVY: Marty, come on, just give it a shot, you can't lose here.

MARTY: How about . . . "Mud Slide Kills Sixty-four in Slums of Chile"?

LEVY: That's good. Triumph over tragedy. Sounds like a John Boorman picture. Slap a happy ending on it, the

script will write itself. Bon, here. Marty, give me the
paper—

(LEVY *hands paper to* BONNIE.)

BONNIE: Gee, I don't know, Lar.

LEVY: Give it a shot.

BONNIE: Okay. "Further Bond Losses Push Dow Jones
Down 7.15." I see Connery as Bond.

(*The camera zooms in on an article in the next column:* "Man
Found Dead in Theater Parking Lot.")

LEVY: That's funny. Good thing Oliver Stone wasn't listen-
ing to you. Where would we have been?

BONNIE: We all would've been spared having to sit
through *Wall Street,* for one thing.

(BONNIE *has tossed the paper down on the table in front of* GRIFFIN. *He
looks down at the paper. Staring up at him is the article. During the
following, he reaches for the paper. He folds it and keeps it.*)

LEVY: Marty. What did *Wall Street* do worldwide?

MARTY: Seventy, seventy-five, maybe eighty million.

LEVY: Eighty million dollars and a couple of Oscars.

LEVISON: Okay, okay. I think Larry's point is well taken.
Griffin, can you give us an update on the Taylor Hack-
ford project?

(GRIFFIN *is staring into space.*)

LEVISON: Griffin?

GRIFFIN: Yeah? I was just thinking what an interesting
concept it is to eliminate the writer from the artistic pro-
cess. If we could just get rid of these actors and directors,
maybe we've got something here.

INTERIOR: GRIFFIN'S INNER OFFICE. DAY.

WALTER *sits at Griffin's desk. He plays with a desk toy.*

GRIFFIN: Hello, Walter. Make yourself at home.

WALTER: Mr. Mill.

(*He gets up, and* GRIFFIN *sits at his desk.*)

WALTER: I understand you were kinda late coming in this
morning. You all right?

GRIFFIN: I'm fine. I appreciate your concern. What can I

do for you, Walter? Don't tell me you came here to pitch me a story.

WALTER: That's exactly what I've come to do. It's a good one, too. About a writer—sort of. David Kahane.

GRIFFIN: David Kahane? Who's David Kahane?

WALTER: Oh, you met him.

GRIFFIN: I meet a lot of writers.

WALTER: Uh-huh. But this particular writer that you met was murdered last night, in back of the Rialto Theater in Pasadena.

GRIFFIN: Murdered?

WALTER: Come to think of it, Pasadena's as good a place to die as any.

GRIFFIN: So what's the story?

WALTER: In twenty-five words or less? Okay. Movie Exec calls writer. Writer's girlfriend says he's at the movies. Exec goes to movies. Meets writer. Drinks with writer. Writer gets konked and dies in four inches of dirty water. Movie Exec is in deep shit. What do you think?

GRIFFIN: That was more than twenty-five words, and it's bullshit.

WALTER: Pasadena homicide doesn't think it's bullshit. They've got a complete report. You met Kahane at the Rialto. You got drunk with him in a Japanese restaurant; he left before you did. That was the last time anybody saw him alive. Except you, maybe. Why are you denying this?

GRIFFIN: What do the police think?

WALTER: They think it was a botched robbery. The window of his car was busted. Surprised someone trying to take the radio. There was a fight. He was killed.

GRIFFIN: I didn't kill him, Walter. I went to see him. I know I said I didn't, but I did.

WALTER: Then why did you lie to me?

GRIFFIN: Well, now's not a very good time for me. Haven't you heard the rumors? I'm on my way out. That's all I need, a little more controversy. It's just not a good time, Walter.

WALTER: Look. I'm in charge of Studio Security in every definition of the word. Which means, it's my job to take care of a studio executive should he be, shall we say, under suspicion of murder at a time when profits are down and the company is vulnerable for a takeover. It's my job to keep this very, very, very, very quiet! Do you wanna help?

GRIFFIN: Of course . . .

WALTER: Then, stop lying. How many meetings did you have with this guy?

GRIFFIN: One.

WALTER: Not counting last night.

GRIFFIN: Not counting last night.

WALTER: Why did you go all the way to Pasadena to meet him?

GRIFFIN: He had an idea I was interested in. I wanted to talk to him about it right away.

WALTER: His girlfriend. I guess she's a friend of yours, too? Think fast!

(WALTER *throws a ball at* GRIFFIN *who barely catches it.*)

GRIFFIN: Jesus, Walter! What is this?

WALTER (*shouting*): It's called the third degree. And if you don't like it, just wait until the cops start asking questions!

GRIFFIN (*angry*): I'll go to the police right now. You come with me!

WALTER: No. They'll come here. You're acting like someone who's guilty. You're not guilty, are you?

GRIFFIN: For the last time, I'm not a murderer.

(*The fax machine in Griffin's office starts humming. Something is coming in. And he looks down at the fax. His point of view: the fax. It is in the form of a postcard. It reads:* "SURPRISE!")

WALTER (*referring to the fax*): Bad news?

GRIFFIN (*looks up*): What?

WALTER: That fax. Is it bad news?

GRIFFIN: No, business as usual.

*   *   *

EXTERIOR: CEMETERY. DAY.
PHIL *stands in front of a group of mourners. He eulogizes* KAHANE.
Griffin's car drives past.

PHIL: The Hollywood system didn't murder David Kahane. Not the ninety-eight-million-dollar movie, not the twelve-million-dollar actor, not even the million-dollar deal that David Kahane never landed. No, the most we can pin on Hollywood is assault with the intent to kill because society is responsible for this particular murder. And it is to society that we must look if we are to have any justice for that crime. Because someone in the night killed David Kahane, and that person will have to bear the guilt. And if David were here right now, I know in my heart that David would say: "Cut the shit, Phil. What did you learn from all this? Did you learn from this?" And I would say, "Yeah, David, I've learned a lot; we here will take it from here." And the next time we sell a script for a million dollars and the next time we nail some shit-bag producer to the wall, we'll say: "That's another one for David Kahane!" David was working on something the day he died. (PHIL *takes a few pages from his inside coat pocket.*) I'd like to share it with you. (*He reads from the screenplay, expressively.*) "Blackness. A mangy dog barks, and garbage can lids are lifted as derelicts in the street hunt for food. Buzzing. As a cheap alarm clock goes off. Interior, flophouse room, early morning. A tracking shot moves through the grimy room. Light streams in through holes in the yellowing window shade. Moths dance in the beams of light. Track down along the floor, the frayed rug. Stop on a shoe. It's empty." (*He puts the paper down.*) That's as far as he got. It's the last thing he wrote. So long, Dave. Fade-out. Thank you.

EXTERIOR: CEMETERY. KAHANE'S FUNERAL SERVICE. DAY.
As PHIL *speaks to the gathering,* GRIFFIN *arrives and remains standing in the back. Mourners sit in chairs facing the grave site. He looks*

for JUNE. *His point of view scans the back of heads looking for her. He stops at a head that might be hers. He sees her. She sits all alone. The service ends.* JUNE *leaves and walks by* GRIFFIN.

JUNE: Who are you? (*A statement not a question:*) You're not a writer.

GRIFFIN: No, I'm not. I'm Griffin Mill. We spoke the night David . . .

JUNE: Blue sea, white sea. It turned out you were right.

GRIFFIN: What?

JUNE: It was a red sea.

(*He doesn't get it for a moment.*)

GRIFFIN: Oh? Yeah.

JUNE: You're the only person I know here.

GRIFFIN: I'm really sorry about David. He was a talent.

JUNE: Do you really think so? I always suspected he was uniquely untalented. It's nice of you to say that. It was nice of you to come. But really you didn't have to.

GRIFFIN: Well, I did. You know, I was probably the last person to see him alive.

JUNE: Yes, the police told me. Well, not quite the last, surely?

GRIFFIN (*shocked for a moment*): Well, no, no but . . . (*His sentence trails off. He tries again.*) I'm sure this is a terrible time for you. Is there anything you need?

JUNE: No. I don't feel bad. It's like when my parents died. I didn't feel anything at all. They were just gone.

GRIFFIN: Well, it probably hasn't sunk in yet.

JUNE: That was years ago.

GRIFFIN: No, I meant David.

JUNE: Oh.

(*Mourners are leaving.*)

JUNE: Oh, God. People. I don't like it here. They all expect me to grieve and mourn, and I can't talk to them. David's gone, and I'm somewhere else already. (*She looks at* GRIFFIN:) Will you take me home?

GRIFFIN: What?

JUNE: Will you take me home?

GRIFFIN: Sure.

(*They prepare to get in Griffin's car.* GRIFFIN *notices* PAUL DE LONGPRE *standing in the back watching him.*)

INTERIOR: JUNE'S LIVING ROOM. DAY.

GRIFFIN *is in the living room alone. There is nothing in the room except June's paintings, paint supplies, and collage material: boxes of broken glass, Saran Wrap, Polaroid film boxes. June's paintings are everywhere—stacked against the wall as well as mounted. They all look like the frozen North, whites and grays. The word* Iceland *in various forms is written on the paintings.* GRIFFIN *is looking at the paintings.*

GRIFFIN: These are really interesting. I like them.

JUNE: Would you like a drink?

GRIFFIN: No thanks. Where do you show?

JUNE: Hmm?

GRIFFIN: Gallery. What gallery? Who's your dealer?

JUNE: I don't have a dealer. I couldn't sell these. They're never finished. Cookie?

GRIFFIN: No thanks. They're never finished?

JUNE: No, they're just what I do, for myself. What I feel. You ask lots of questions, Mr. Mill. You're just like the police. That's all they did. Ask questions. They asked me a lot about you.

GRIFFIN: Did they?

JUNE: How long we'd known each other. If you'd ever been to the house before . . .

GRIFFIN: Well, I suppose they have to ask those questions . . .

JUNE: I don't see why.

GRIFFIN: 'Cause that's what the police do.

JUNE: Can I ask you a question? (*She picks up her Polaroid camera.*) Why was it so important to see David that night? (*She snaps his picture.*) What was so urgent?

GRIFFIN: Oh, um, well, he had pitched me a story a few months ago.

JUNE: The Japan story.

(*She takes another picture.*)

GRIFFIN: Yeah, the Japan story. Well, I liked it at the time, but it needed work. Especially the ending. And, I was sitting at my desk that day, and it suddenly occurred to me. How to make the ending work.

JUNE (*looking at him intently*): So, what was it?

GRIFFIN: What?

JUNE: Your idea for the ending.

GRIFFIN: Up.

(*She takes another picture.* GRIFFIN *looks at the camera.*)

JUNE: Up? What does that mean?

GRIFFIN: Up as opposed to down. Moods. You know, happy as opposed to sad. Hopeful as opposed to depressing. What did you think of his ending?

(*She keeps taking Polaroid photographs.*)

JUNE: I never read it.

GRIFFIN: You never read it?

JUNE: No. I don't like reading.

GRIFFIN: Do you like books?

JUNE: I like words. And letters, but I'm not crazy about complete sentences. So what did he think?

GRIFFIN: He walked out on me, actually. I don't think David liked me very much.

JUNE: I think he just didn't like happy endings. Put your face here.

(*She takes his picture.*)

GRIFFIN: What are you doing? You're not going to paint me, are you?

JUNE: I might put you in one of my paintings. There's one that I want to do of an Icelandic hero. He's a thief and made of fire. But you might not like that.

GRIFFIN: Why not?

JUNE: Because you're in the movies, and you can't have thieves as heroes. Can you?

GRIFFIN: Well, I don't know about that. We have a long tradition of gangsters in the movies.

JUNE: Yes, but they always have to suffer for their crimes, don't they?

GRIFFIN: We should pay for our crimes, shouldn't we?

JUNE: Oh, I don't know. I think, knowing that you committed the crime is suffering enough. And if you don't suffer from it, maybe it wasn't a crime after all. Anyway, what difference does it make? It has nothing to do with how things really are.

GRIFFIN: You don't really believe that, do you?

JUNE: Oh, I don't know what I believe, Mr. Mill. It's just the way I feel.

GRIFFIN: Do you know what you are, June whatever-your-name-is? You're a pragmatic anarchist.

JUNE: Is that what I am? I never was sure.

(GRIFFIN *picks up the Polaroid and takes a picture of her.*)

INTERIOR: GRIFFIN'S OFFICE. DAY.

Detectives SUSAN AVERY *and her assistant,* WILLA BROOM (*late thirties*), *examine an Oscar statue.* WALTER *watches.*

AVERY: Can I pick this up?

(WALTER *nods. She picks up the statue.*)

AVERY: Yeah? Oh, heavy—

WALTER: Thirty-seven ounces.

AVERY: Really? Oh, look, look. I'd like to thank my mother, and her mother, and her father's mother who was the—

(GRIFFIN *enters. She is a little impressed with* GRIFFIN *but only a little.*)

GRIFFIN: Hello . . .

AVERY (*putting statue down*): Oh.

WALTER: This is Detective Susan Avery.

AVERY: How do you do. This is my partner—

WILLA: Willa Broom.

GRIFFIN: A pleasure. Let's go in here.

(*They move into* GRIFFIN'S *inner office. Outside,* DE LONGPRE *paces in the parking lot.*)

WALTER (*to* GRIFFIN): This is the first real movie studio Detective Avery's been to.

AVERY: Well, aside from the Universal tour. You know, when my family comes, I always take them out there. I've been out there so often, I kinda feel I'm ready to direct.

WALTER: Probably do better than most of the film grads they're handing the cameras to these days.

GRIFFIN (*taking the bull by the horns*): Listen, I'm sorry I didn't call you as soon as I heard that Kahane was dead.

AVERY: Heard or read?

GRIFFIN: Read.

AVERY: Why didn't you?

GRIFFIN: Walter asked me the same question. I wish I had a better answer for you, but all I can say is, I didn't think about it.

AVERY: Hmm. How did you know where he was going to be?

GRIFFIN: His wife told me he was seeing *The Bicycle Thief* . . .

WILLA: Girlfriend.

AVERY: Girlfriend.

GRIFFIN: Girlfriend. I didn't know either of them. I was feeling restless, so I thought I'd go see the movie, and if he was there, I'd talk to him about a job I thought he was good for.

AVERY: So, you got to the theater, you saw him, and?

GRIFFIN: We went and had a drink, this Japanese place he knew, this wild, incredible scene, it was like Tokyo.

AVERY (*not impressed with his enthusiasm*): He left before you did. Why didn't you leave together?

GRIFFIN: I told you, it was an incredible scene. I was having a great time.

AVERY: Then why didn't you stay longer?

GRIFFIN: Well, people stopped singing, and then it was just a bar. And I don't drink.

AVERY: You drank with him.

GRIFFIN: Well, when in Rome.

AVERY: Did you know him socially?

GRIFFIN: No.

AVERY: Been to his house?

GRIFFIN: No.

AVERY: Did you know anything about him personally?

GRIFFIN: No.

(WALTER *shoots his cuffs and claps his hands.*)

WALTER: Griffin, guess I'm going to let you get back to work now.

(*Everyone gets up.* GRIFFIN *can sense Avery's dissatisfaction.*)

GRIFFIN: Something's bothering you, what is it?

AVERY: Well, I just have to ask you. Did you see him in the parking lot after you left?

GRIFFIN: No, I parked on the street. I drive a Range Rover, so I always feel safer when it's visible. Out on the street, who's going to smash the window?

AVERY: You mean if you had a shitty car you would have been parked in a parking lot?

GRIFFIN: If I had a shitty car, I might be a dead man.

AVERY: Somehow, I think you're too lucky for that. Thank you.

INTERIOR: HOTEL ROOM. NIGHT.

A slate is pulled away. A neon sign flashes outside. LILY TOMLIN, *as Dolores, paces the room smoking a cigarette.* SCOTT GLENN, *as Jake, sits on the bed, talking on the telephone. He's in his shirt-sleeves. There's a gun holstered under his arm.*

VOICE (*offscreen*): Take three, mark . . . Action!

SCOTT GLENN (*into the phone*): No, goddamn it, Peterson. You listen to me: I've been around a while, and I've got a nose. This situation stinks. It stinks of "The Company." That's right, Peterson, the fucking CIA, ever heard of it? This is just the sort of operation those whiz-kid fucks with white shirts—

INTERIOR: SCREENING ROOM. DAY.

The Lonely Room *dailies. The production staff watches.* LEVISON *sits next to* GRIFFIN. BONNIE *and* LEVY *argue across the aisle about the director.*

BONNIE: You just don't understand what he's trying to go for here.

LEVY: I guess I don't.

BONNIE: I find it hard to listen to your argument when you don't—you don't even understand what he's going for.

SCOTT GLENN (*to* LILY TOMLIN): You wanna shut up, please?

LEVY: It's impossible for anyone else to tell what he's going for, because you can't even see anything.

LILY TOMLIN (*as herself*): Oh, kiss my ass. I have to cut because my robe caught on the drawer here.

SCOTT GLENN (*as himself*): Oh, for Christ's sake!

(SANDY *creeps up the aisle taking drink orders from the team.*)

GRIFFIN: Can I have some Volvic, please?

ON-SCREEN.

SCOTT GLENN (*on the phone*): No, goddamn it, Peterson.

IN SCREENING ROOM.

The dailies continue as LEVISON *and* GRIFFIN *speak across the aisle.*

LEVISON: I heard the police came to see you about this dead writer. Who was this guy?

GRIFFIN: His name was David Kahane.

LEVISON: I never heard of him. Did we ever hire him for anything?

GRIFFIN: I was thinking about it. He pitched me a story. I went out there to talk to him about it.

LEVISON: Jesus. Poor bastard. Just when his ship is about to come in, some black kid wants his money for crack.

ON SCREEN.

SCOTT GLENN (*to* LILY TOMLIN): We can't do this. I'm sorry. I don't want to criticize you, baby, but I'm supposed to be having a conversation on the phone.

LILY TOMLIN: Are you talking to me?

IN SCREENING ROOM.

LEVISON (*to* GRIFFIN): Aiee. Creepy. Are the cops still bothering you?

GRIFFIN (*to* LEVISON): No. I don't think so.

LEVISON (*to* GRIFFIN): Well, let Stuckel handle it. He'll give them a couple passes to a screening where they can sit two rows behind Michelle Pfeiffer, and they'll leave you alone.

(JAN *comes in. She goes to* GRIFFIN.)

JAN: Griffin?

GRIFFIN (*to* JAN): What's up?

JAN: A guy named Joe Gillis called. He said he'd meet you at the St. James Club at ten o'clock on the patio. Griffin, who's Joe Gillis?

GRIFFIN: Joe Gillis? Never heard of him.

JAN: He said you'd know.

GRIFFIN (*to the group*): Anyone know who Joe Gillis is?

LEVISON: He's the character that William Holden played in *Sunset Boulevard*. The writer who gets killed by the movie star.

BONNIE (*to* GRIFFIN): Gloria Swanson.

GRIFFIN (*sort of laughing*): Oh. Oh yeah, I know who that guy is. Last week he said he was Charles Foster Kane. The week before that, it was Rhett Butler.

ON-SCREEN.

LILY TOMLIN: How can they think I'd kill my own sister's husband? I was in love with him.

EXTERIOR/INTERIOR: ST. JAMES CLUB. NIGHT.

GRIFFIN *drives to the hotel entrance. He leaves his car with the valet. He is on his guard. There are people in the lobby. Which one is the* POSTCARD WRITER?

MALCOLM MCDOWELL *and a friend are checking out of the hotel.*

MALCOLM MCDOWELL: Griffin! Griffin.

GRIFFIN: Malcolm McDowell.

MALCOLM MCDOWELL: How are you? (*Suddenly, rage.*) Listen, next time you want to bad-mouth me, have the courage to do it to my face! You guys are all the same.

(*He leaves.* GRIFFIN *goes to the bar.* ANDY CIVELLA *and* TOM OAKLEY *are sitting in the lounge with* ANDIE MCDOWELL. *When* ANDY CIVELLA *sees* GRIFFIN, *he leaps up.*)

OAKLEY: . . . It ended with Cimino and *Heaven's Gate*.

CIVELLA: Griffin Mill! Hi! Andy Civella!

GRIFFIN: Hi. How are you?

CIVELLA: I've got Andie McDowell sitting over here. You know her. She's so hot.

GRIFFIN: You still living in New York?

CIVELLA: I couldn't live here, I'm allergic to happiness. Griffin, Andie McDowell.

GRIFFIN (*to* ANDIE McDOWELL): Hello.

CIVELLA: She's my namesake. She's the smart Andie, and I'm the pretty one. And you geniuses know each other, Tom Oakley.

GRIFFIN: Oh, yes. Hi, Tom. It's funny, I just ran into *Malcolm* McDowell in the lobby.

OAKLEY: Roddy McDowell's related to a cousin of my brother-in-law.

ANDIE McDOWELL: Well, I'm afraid I'm not related to either of them.

(GRIFFIN *sees* DE LONGPRE *enter the hotel and walk up the steps.* GRIFFIN *is distracted.*)

OAKLEY: . . . If I write it, I direct it.

CIVELLA: The last three pictures you directed were bombs!

(ANDIE McDOWELL *stands when a friend arrives.*)

ANDIE McDOWELL: Thank you so much for the drink. We have to go.

CIVELLA: You have to go? We'll walk you to the car.

ANDIE McDOWELL: No, that's okay.

(ANDIE McDOWELL *and her friend leave.*)

CIVELLA: Griffin, Griffin, we'd like to buy you a drink.

GRIFFIN: I'm sorry, I can't. I'm meeting someone. Business.

(GRIFFIN *heads for the patio.*)

OAKLEY (*to* CIVELLA): We should tell him about *Habeas Corpus.*

CIVELLA: Of course, of course, but he's a busy man.

(GRIFFIN *approaches the* MAÎTRE D' *as they leave.*)

GRIFFIN: Is there anyone waiting for me?

MAÎTRE D': No one's asked.

GRIFFIN: I'm expecting someone. I'll be out by the pool.

CIVELLA: But he'll get back to us. Right, Griffin? Andie?

(CIVELLA *and* OAKLEY *chase after* ANDIE MCDOWELL.
DE LONGPRE *goes to the bar.*)

EXTERIOR: PATIO. NIGHT.

GRIFFIN *sits down at a table. He studies the patio. No one looks like a writer.* GRIFFIN *feels exhausted. He orders a mineral water. Suddenly, a hand rests on his shoulder. He jumps and turns. It is* CIVELLA.

CIVELLA: Oh, sorry, sorry.

GRIFFIN: Jesus, Andy. It's you.

CIVELLA: Of course, it's me.

(CIVELLA *moves over and sits across from* GRIFFIN. GRIFFIN *is very annoyed that* CIVELLA *is there.*)

GRIFFIN: Listen, I can't ask you to join me. I told you, I'm meeting somebody.

CIVELLA: Yeah, you're meeting me. We've got some big business.

(CIVELLA *smiles at him, knowingly.*)

GRIFFIN (*suddenly realizing*): You?! You?!

(GRIFFIN *jumps up, distraught.*)

CIVELLA (*grins*): Why not me?

GRIFFIN: Jesus Christ, Andy. You think this is funny? You think this is fucking funny?

CIVELLA: What are you talking about?

(OAKLEY *walks into the patio area to join them.*)

OAKLEY: Wouldn't she make a great Nora? God, I'd love to write another *Doll's House* for her.

CIVELLA: Did you meet Tom Oakley?

GRIFFIN: Yeah, you mean you didn't call me?

CIVELLA: No, I didn't call you.

(GRIFFIN *realizes he's made a big mistake.*)

GRIFFIN: I'm sorry, I'm really sorry. Listen, I really am meeting somebody. There's no way I can hear a pitch right now. You'll have to call me tomorrow.

(*Civella's beeper goes off.*)

CIVELLA: No, I can't do it tomorrow. I've got a meeting at Paramount, and I've got a meeting at Universal too . . .

GRIFFIN: Congratulations—

CIVELLA: . . . In the morning, and if you don't hear it now, you're gonna lose it.

GRIFFIN: Well, then, I lose it, all right?

CIVELLA: It'll take twenty seconds. When your friend gets here—

GRIFFIN: What friend? What are you talking about?

CIVELLA (*panicked by Griffin's hostility*): Whoever you are going to meet here.

(GRIFFIN *consents and sits down.* OAKLEY *sits across the table.*)

GRIFFIN: Twenty-five words or less.

CIVELLA: Absolutely. Tom, no, you sit here, go!

(OAKLEY *switches seats with* CIVELLA.)

OAKLEY: A district attorney is at a moral crossroads . . .

CIVELLA: Jesus Christ, Tom . . .

OAKLEY: Okay, okay. We open outside the largest penitentiary in California. It's night, it's raining. A limousine comes in through the front gate, past a tight knot of demonstrators holding a candlelight vigil. The candles under the umbrellas make them glow like Japanese lanterns . . .

GRIFFIN: That's nice. I haven't seen that before. That's good.

OAKLEY: A lone demonstrator, a black woman, steps in front of the limousine. The lights illuminate her like a spirit. Her eyes fix upon those of the sole passenger. The moment is devastating between them.

GRIFFIN: He's the district attorney, and she's the mother of the person that's being executed.

CIVELLA: You're *good.* (*To* OAKLEY:) See, I told you he's good . . .

GRIFFIN: Go on.

OAKLEY: Okay, the D.A. believes in the death penalty. And the execution is a hard case, black, nineteen, and definitely guilty. We're the greatest democracy in the world, and 36 percent of the people on death row are black.

CIVELLA: More, more!

OAKLEY: Poor, disadvantaged, black. And he swears, the next person he sees die is going to be smart, rich, and white! You . . . Me . . .

CIVELLA: What a hook, huh? Beauty hook. Cut to the chase, Tom.

OAKLEY: Cut from the D.A. to an upmarket suburban neighborhood. A couple have a fight. He leaves in a fit, gets in a car. It's the same rainy night. The car spins out on the road and goes into a ravine. The body is swept away. Now, when the police examine the car, they find the brakes have been tampered with. It's murder. And the D.A. decides to go for the big one, and he's going to put the wife in the gas chamber.

GRIFFIN: But—the D.A. falls in love with the wife.

OAKLEY: But, of course, he falls in love with the wife, but he puts her in the gas chamber anyway. Then, he finds out the husband is alive! That he faked his death. The D.A. breaks into the prison, runs down death row, but— he gets there too late. The gas pellets have been dropped. She's *dead*. I tell you, there's not a dry eye in the house.

GRIFFIN: She's dead?

OAKLEY: She's dead. She's dead, because that's the reality! The innocent die.

GRIFFIN: Who's the D.A.?

OAKLEY: Ah! No one.

GRIFFIN: No one?

OAKLEY: No stars on this project. We're going out on a limb on this one.

CIVELLA: You know, like unknowns. Stage actors. Or maybe somebody English. Like what's-his-name.

GRIFFIN: Why?

OAKLEY: Why? why? Because this story is just too damned important to risk being overwhelmed by personality. That's fine for action pictures, but this is special. We want real people here. We don't want people coming into this with any preconceived notions. We want them to see a district attorney.

CIVELLA (*confidentially to* GRIFFIN, *casting the movie*): Bruce Willis . . .

OAKLEY: No, not Bruce Willis. Not Kevin Costner. This is an innocent woman fighting for her life.

CIVELLA/GRIFFIN (entre nous): Julia Roberts.

GRIFFIN: If we can get her—

CIVELLA: Of course, we can get her.

OAKLEY: If I'm perfectly honest, if I think about this, this isn't even an American film.

GRIFFIN: It's not?

OAKLEY: No, there are no stars, no pat happy endings, no Schwarzenegger stickups, no terrorists. This is a tough story—a tragedy—in which an innocent woman dies. Why? Because that happens.

(*Civella's beeper goes off.*)

CIVELLA: *Habeas Corpus*. That's what we're calling it. Produce the corpse. What do you say? Yes or no?

GRIFFIN: That pitch was more than twenty-five words.

CIVELLA: Yeah, but it's brilliant. What's the verdict, Griffin?

(*The* WAITER *comes to the table.*)

WAITER: Mr. Mill, for you.

(*He gives* GRIFFIN *a postcard.*)

GRIFFIN: Who gave this to you?

WAITER: I received it at the front desk.

(GRIFFIN *reads the message.* "I said to come alone." *It's addressed:* Griffin Mill, St. James Club. *The illustration: a rattlesnake, Death Valley.*)

OAKLEY: What is it?

GRIFFIN: It's, um, from the person I was meeting. He's not coming.

(GRIFFIN *gets up to leave. His mind is elsewhere.*)

CIVELLA: Well, do we have a shot?

GRIFFIN: It's an intriguing idea. Give me a call at the studio tomorrow.

CIVELLA: Yeah!

OAKLEY: Okay. There's a scene in *Throne of Blood* that has exactly the texture, if you will.

CIVELLA: Tom, just say thank you.

OAKLEY: She has to die, no fucking Hollywood ending.

CIVELLA: Tom, say thank you.

(GRIFFIN *leaves.*)

EXTERIOR: ST. JAMES CLUB. NIGHT.

GRIFFIN *hands his parking ticket to the valet. He tips the valet and gets in.*

The shadow's point of view watches GRIFFIN *drive away.*

INTERIOR: GRIFFIN'S CAR. NIGHT.

GRIFFIN *drives down Sunset Boulevard.*

He drives into Beverly Hills. A telephone rings in the car. The car's fax is receiving a transmission. A page comes out. A simple message: "LOOK UNDER YOUR RAINCOAT." GRIFFIN *looks under his raincoat, revealing a magician's box and a note:* "Don't Open Till Xmas." *He opens the box. A rattlesnake is inside. The snake shakes its rattle, and it coils, ready to spring.* GRIFFIN *swerves across the road. He pulls into an alley, gets out, takes off his shirt, pulls an umbrella out of the back of his car, opens the passenger door, drops his shirt on the snake, and then beats it to death.*

GRIFFIN: Fucking dog-shit writer! You fucking try to kill me?

(*He pulls the snake from the car.*)

INTERIOR: JUNE'S HOUSE. NIGHT.

JUNE *is painting. Griffin's Polaroid image is in the painting. She works for awhile and then goes to get something near a window. She sees Griffin's face staring at her. It startles her.*

JUNE: Oh, my God! You gave me such a scare. What are you doing here? You gave me such a fright. Come in. Come on in.

(*He leaves the window, and she goes to open the front door. She lets him in.*)

JUNE: What's the matter? You look terrible. What's up? Sit down, I'll get you a drink.

(*He sits as she goes to the fridge and takes out a bottle of vodka. She pours him a drink.*)

JUNE: What happened?

GRIFFIN: Is it too late? I'm sorry . . .

JUNE: No, no, no. It's not too late. No.

GRIFFIN: I don't even know what time it is.

JUNE: What's wrong?

GRIFFIN: What are you painting? Is that me?

JUNE: Yes. That's you. See?

GRIFFIN: Do they have snakes in Iceland?

JUNE: Snakes? I don't think so.

GRIFFIN: Are you afraid of snakes?

JUNE: I don't know. I've never been close to a real one.

GRIFFIN: They scare the shit out of me.

JUNE: Have another.

GRIFFIN: I don't usually drink.

(*She pours him another drink.*)

JUNE: Did something happen tonight?

GRIFFIN: Yes, but, there's something else I have to tell you.

JUNE: Yes?

GRIFFIN: This isn't easy for me.

(*They stare at each other for a moment. Finally, she speaks:*)

JUNE: Yes . . . How about if I get on with my work, and you just talk to me when you feel like it? Okay?

(*She goes back to her work.*)

GRIFFIN: I came very close to dying tonight. (*She listens.*) All I thought about was you. I don't even know you, and you came into my mind, and I couldn't, I couldn't think of anything else. Remember that first night we spoke . . . on the phone? Well, I was outside these windows watching you, you know. It was so exciting and so new and strange. I can't get you out of my mind.

JUNE: Are you making love to me?

(*He hadn't thought of that.*)

> GRIFFIN: Yes. I guess I am. I guess I am. I want to make love to you. I want to make love to you.

(*She doesn't move for a bit.*)

> JUNE: It's too soon. It's too soon. Isn't it? It's so strange how things happen? So strange. David was here, then he left, you arrived. Maybe it's the timing, but I feel like I would go anywhere with you, if you asked. But we mustn't hurry things. We can't hurry things, any more than we can stop them. (*She is close to tears.*) You'd better go now. I think I'm going to cry now. Better go. Quick.

(*She opens the door.*)

> GRIFFIN: I'm sorry.

> JUNE: No, no, no. Don't be sorry. Just go home and get some sleep, and call me, tomorrow. Invite me on a proper date. I'd like that . . .

(*He leaves, and she closes the door.*)

INTERIOR: GRIFFIN'S INNER OFFICE. DAY.
From the poster: Highly Dangerous.

INTERIOR: GRIFFIN'S INNER OFFICE. DAY.

> GRIFFIN: Jan, Jan! Get me Larry Levy on the phone.

> JAN (*offscreen*): I don't think he's on the lot.

(GRIFFIN, OAKLEY, *and* CIVELLA *are around Griffin's desk.*)

> OAKLEY: Isn't he at Fox?

> GRIFFIN: He used to be. Not anymore.

> OAKLEY: I pitched him something a few months ago, and he hated it.

(*A moment in the room as they wait. A buzz:* LEVY *is on the line.*)

EXTERIOR: LEVY'S CAR IN CENTURY CITY. DAY.
As LEVY *drives, he talks to* GRIFFIN *on his car's speaker phone. He drives a Mercedes.*

Levy: Griffin.

Griffin (*voice-over*): Larry, I've got Andy Civella and Tom Oakley here, and I wouldn't be bothering you if I didn't think they had an idea that you should hear right away.

Levy: Hi, guys.

Civella (*voice-over*): Hi, Larry. Listen, the next voice you hear will have an English accent. Tom Oakley. I'm Andy Civella.

Levy: Hi, Andy. I know Tom. How are you, Tom?

Oakley (*voice-over*): Very well, Larry, and yourself?

Levy: Fine. What's your story?

(Oakley *is confident.*)

Oakley (*voice-over*): We open outside San Quentin. It's night. It's raining. A limousine enters through the front gate, past a small knot of demonstrators holding a candlelight vigil. The candles are flickering underneath the umbrellas, make them glow like Japanese lanterns. A lone demonstrator, a black woman, steps in front of the limousine. Her eyes connect with the lone passenger. It's a devastating moment . . .

(Levy *listens as he cruises down road.*)

INTERIOR: GRIFFIN'S INNER OFFICE. LATE AFTERNOON.

Oakley (*into the speaker phone*): . . . No stars, no Schwarzenegger, no pat Hollywood endings, no car chases. This is an American tragedy in which an innocent woman dies, because that happens. That's reality.

(Oakley *sinks back into his chair, drained from the passion of his pitch.*)

EXTERIOR: LEVY'S CAR IN BEVERLY HILLS. DAY.

Levy *is on the phone in his car.*

Levy: Take me off the speaker phone, Griffin.

* * *

INTERIOR: GRIFFIN'S OFFICE. LATE AFTERNOON.
GRIFFIN *pushes a button and picks up the receiver.*
> GRIFFIN: Yeah.

EXTERIOR: LEVY'S CAR. LATE AFTERNOON.
> LEVY (*voice-over*): I don't know. It's a really hot story, but
> what is this bullshit, "no stars"?
> GRIFFIN (*voice-over*): Let me give you a little tip, Larry.
> Levison came to power on two movies, and they made
> three hundred million, and they had no stars. He's going
> to love this idea. It'll remind him of his youth. Do you
> know what his motto used to be? No stars, just talent.

INTERIOR: LEVY'S CAR. LATE AFTERNOON.
LEVY *is in his car. That convinces him.*
> LEVY: Has anyone else heard this?
> GRIFFIN (*voice-over*): I don't think so, no.
> LEVY: We should make a deal now. Tomorrow may be
> too late. Can we get a hold of Levison?
> GRIFFIN (*voice-over*): Yeah, I'll get Levison. When can you
> be back?
> LEVY: I'll be there right after my A.A. meeting.
> GRIFFIN (*voice-over*): Oh, Larry, I didn't realize you had a
> drinking problem.
> LEVY: Well, I don't, really. But that's where all the deals
> are being made these days. See ya!
(*Cut to:*)

INTERIOR: GRIFFIN'S OUTER OFFICE. LATER.
CIVELLA, OAKLEY, *and* GRIFFIN *come out of the inner office, all smiles.*
GRIFFIN *shows them out.*
> GRIFFIN: Tom, that was a hell of a pitch. Good work. I
> think you sold Larry.

CIVELLA: Great! When are we going to hear?

GRIFFIN: I want you to go home. I want you to put the champagne on ice, and I'll give you an answer by tonight. (*Into the intercom:*) Jan, come on in here.

CIVELLA: Griffin, you move in mysterious ways. But I like it. I like it.

OAKLEY: Did Levy understand *NO STARS?*

GRIFFIN: Yes, he was *particularly* attracted by that notion.

OAKLEY (*over his shoulder*): And no Hollywood ending.

GRIFFIN: No Hollywood ending.

(*They leave as* JAN *enters.*)

JAN: They looked happy.

GRIFFIN: They have a completely fucked-up idea that has no second act. If I hadn't heard it myself, I never would have believed it. Larry Levy liked it because he's a dick brain. Levy will sell the idea to Levison, and then I'll let Levison have the brilliant idea of letting Larry take over the project from me.

JAN: You will?

GRIFFIN: You see, Levison can't wait to get in bed with Levy. This piece of shit will blow up in both of their faces, and I will step in and save the day.

(*He throws a basketball into an executive hoop.*)

BASKETBALL: Score! Three points! Great catch!

(*Outside,* DETECTIVE DE LONGPRE *talks to* JIMMY *in the parking lot.*)

INTERIOR: LEVISON'S BUNGALOW. EVENING.

LEVY; LEVISON; BONNIE; *Bonnie's assistant,* WHITNEY; GRIFFIN. LEVY *has just finished pitching* Habeas Corpus *to* LEVISON.

LEVY: She's receiving the last rites. The D.A. discovers the husband faked his own death, she's innocent, he races to the penitentiary, but it's too late, the pellets are dropped, she's dead . . . He helped kill the woman he loved.

LEVISON (*first question*): Who are the stars?

LEVY: No stars, just talent.

LEVISON: No stars? And what the fuck kind of ending do you call that? It's depressing. It'll bring everybody down.

LEVY: Depressing? Joel! What about *Terms of Endearment? Love Story? Steel Magnolias?* Joel, *E.T.* grossed, what, Marty? Three hundred nineteen million dollars worldwide, precassette, and there wasn't a dry eye in the house. Depressing, I don't think so.

LEVISON: Yeah, but . . .

LEVY: Listen, normally I'd agree with you, but this is an entirely different kind of deal here. It's a matter of taking a risk. Rolling the dice. But if they come up seven, bingo. It's Oscar time.

LEVISON: Do they screw?

LEVY: Who?

LEVISON: The D.A., whoever it is. And the woman. Do they screw? If I'm going to be looking at jail cells and gas chambers, we're going to have to have a little *sex* in this picture.

LEVY: Yeah. Sure. Of course. We'll get it in, no problem.

LEVISON: Okay. Who's going to shepherd this thing? Larry, you seem to have a good feel for this. You want to run with it?

BONNIE (*stepping in*): Wait a minute, Joel. This project originated with Griffin.

GRIFFIN: Bonnie . . .

LEVY: No, no. I don't want to dance at somebody else's wedding. If this is Griffin's project, it's Griffin's project.

BONNIE: I just think—

LEVISON: Bonnie, this will have to be my call.

GRIFFIN (*a calculated pause*): Fine with me. My plate is full anyway. Larry, it's yours. Hit a home run. Win an Oscar for the home team.

(BONNIE *looks at* GRIFFIN.)

LEVISON: Griffin, I've got something else for you.

GRIFFIN: Yeah?

LEVISON: New York. Tomorrow. Tom Wolfe's new book

will be in a room at the Sherry Netherland. You go in, read it, you make your bid.

GRIFFIN: Send Bonnie. She'll know if it's a movie or not. If it is, we know the bid. A million.

(*The phone rings.*)

BONNIE: Me?

LEVY: A million? Oh, that's kind of high, isn't it?

GRIFFIN: It's Tom Wolfe. (*To* BONNIE:) Why not you?

(LEVISON *picks up the phone.*)

LEVISON: Yeah? Who? Hold on.

GRIFFIN: Why not you?

BONNIE: Griffin, I'm a story editor. That's a vice-president's job.

GRIFFIN: You don't want to be a vice-president?

LEVISON: Bonnie, pack your bags.

WHITNEY (*quietly, kissing up to* LEVY): Congratulations, that was the most amazing pitch I ever heard—

BONNIE: What about the museum party?

GRIFFIN: Listen, if you don't want the responsibility . . .

BONNIE: No, I'm going, I'm going.

WHITNEY (*still to* LEVY:) I really want to be one of your soldiers.

LEVY: I'm glad you're on the team, believe me.

WHITNEY: And really, and Bonnie's going to be gone, I'm here for you.

BONNIE: Whitney . . . Whitney, *now!*

LEVISON: Frank, Marty, want to come in?

INTERIOR: STUDIO FOYER. DAY.

BONNIE *stops* GRIFFIN.

BONNIE: May I have a word with you, please?

(*He looks at his watch.*)

GRIFFIN: I've got a meeting.

BONNIE: Yeah, well, find the time. What is going on?

GRIFFIN: What do you mean?

BONNIE: I mean handing Larry Levy your project like that.

GRIFFIN: I just thought Larry had a firm grasp on the style of the piece.

BONNIE: The only thing Larry Levy has a firm grasp on is his dick, and you know it.

GRIFFIN: Come on, Bonnie. I'm not Oz. I can't do everything. If I think Larry has what it takes to get a picture made, why shouldn't I use him? That way, everybody wins.

BONNIE: Why are you bullshitting me? You never used to bullshit me.

GRIFFIN: I'm not bullshitting you.

BONNIE: Yes, you are. Griffin, I know you. I know you. You've been stringing me along like one—

(LEVY *passes behind them.*)

LEVY: *Habeas Corpus!* Griffin, *Habeas Corpus.*

BONNIE: You've been stringing me along like one of your goddamned writers. What is this getting Levison to send me to New York? Are you trying to get rid of me?

GRIFFIN: Trying to get rid of you? I'm trying to help you. If you score in New York, Levison will have to make you a vice-president. Jesus, Bonnie, what's the matter? You afraid of success?

BONNIE: Are you seeing someone else?

GRIFFIN: Oh, this is what this is about?

BONNIE: It's not just this. It's a lot of things. The way you've been acting lately. Something's going on, and I want to know what it is.

GRIFFIN: Jesus Christ, Bonnie.

BONNIE: You're not even looking at me when you're talking to me, Griffin. I want you just to look at me, please look at me right in the eyes and just tell me—no bullshit—and tell me. Is there someone else?

(GRIFFIN *looks her right in the eyes.*)

GRIFFIN: No. (*He kisses her.*) Have a good trip.

*   *   *

EXTERIOR: MUSEUM ENTRANCE. NIGHT.

Entertainment Tonight *over-dub as cars, limousines, and movie stars arrive:* CHER *and* LEVY, NICK NOLTE *and his wife,* ELLIOT GOULD *and his wife,* GRIFFIN *and* JUNE.

> LEEZA GIBBONS: Our top story this evening involves Hollywood's three favorite G's. A glamorous, glitzy, gala night on the town. It is a who's who of stars, no IDs necessary, household names one and all.

INTERIOR: MUSEUM MEZZANINE. NIGHT.

As GRIFFIN *walks through the crowd, he is greeted by people every step of the way. This is his world; these are his people:* TERI GARR, BUCK HENRY, MALCOLM MCDOWELL. *We watch* JUNE *watching him. He's smooth, he's popular. TV crews interview stars as they enter.*

> LEEZA GIBBONS: Leeza Gibbons reporting here, and right this minute, you could fire a cannon down Sunset Boulevard and not come close to hitting a celebrity. Everybody who is anybody is right here. Rubbing elbows and making big talk right here in this ballroom. All the movers, all the shakers, behind the scenes and on the screens. We'll leave it to Cher to wear fire-engine red when the impossible-to-come-by invitations call for black-and-white-only-please.

INTERIOR: COCKTAIL AREA.

People from the studio mill about. SALLY KIRKLAND, JAMES COBURN, MIMI ROGERS, KAREN BLACK *are there.* DE LONGPRE *is there too.*

> GRIFFIN: Hi, Teri, nice to see you. June Gudsmundsdottir, Teri Garr, Buck Henry.

> LEEZA GIBBONS: And the occasion of the evening. Just as big and important as the all-star turnout. The studio world famous for its slogan "Movies, Now More than Ever" is donating prints of twenty-five of its classic black-and-white films to the museum. Now they'll be able to say "Movies, Now More than Ever, Forever."

* * *

INTERIOR: DINNER AREA.

LEVISON *takes the microphone. He is drunk.*

> LEVISON: It's wonderful to see so many familiar and friendly faces around. As you know, the L.A. County Museum has always been close to our hearts and especially the Motion Department, uh, the Motion Picture Department. We are happy to make possible this donation. Now, I'd like to introduce the man whose idea this all was. Griffin Mill, please.

(Applause. GRIFFIN *takes the podium as* LEVISON *takes his seat.* JUNE *is wowed.)*

> GRIFFIN: Thank you, Joel. Grab another drink.

(Laughter.)

> GRIFFIN: I'd like to extend my thanks to the patrons of the Los Angeles County Museum. You have long fostered the ART of motion pictures as a serious and valuable art form in this community. Many people across the country, and around the world, have, for too long, thought of MOVIES as a popular entertainment more than serious ART. And I'm afraid a large majority of the press supports this attitude. We want GREAT films with long shelf lives. We want the films of the new John Hustons, Orson Welleses, Frank Capras. We, and the other major film studios, have a responsibility to the public, to maintain the ART of motion pictures as our primary mandate. MOVIES are ART, now more than ever. Thank you.

(He returns to his seat. Applause.)

> LEVY: That was a hell of a job, Griffin. I couldn't have done it better myself.
>
> CHER: He'll know all of your lines soon. Well, are we having fun yet?

*(*GRIFFIN *finds a postcard under his plate. It says:* "I'll get back to you." *Dance music begins. Looking up, he sees* DE LONGPRE *watching him from across the room.)*

> VOICE *(offscreen)*: So where did you meet?

JUNE: At the funeral. Isn't that right?

GRIFFIN: Absolutely, excuse us.

(GRIFFIN *and* JUNE *get up to dance.*)

LEVISON: Steve, whose daughter is he with? Seriously. She said she was someone's daughter.

(GRIFFIN *and* JUNE *dance.*)

EXTERIOR: JUNE'S HOUSE. NIGHT.

A limousine drives up and stops in front of June's house. JUNE *and* GRIFFIN *are giggling in the backseat. They realize the limousine has stopped.*

JUNE: Don't make a scene.

GRIFFIN: Here we go . . .

(*They get out of the car. He walks her to the front door.*
DETECTIVE DE LONGPRE *watches from his car.*
Under the porch light, she puts her key in the door and unlocks it. She turns back to him.)

JUNE: Now, that's what I call a real date.

(GRIFFIN *kisses her.*)

GRIFFIN: Should I come in?

JUNE: Uh, well . . .

GRIFFIN: Uh well . . .

JUNE: Not tonight.

GRIFFIN: Not tonight.

(*She kisses him.*)

JUNE: But soon. Very soon.

GRIFFIN: How about Mexico?

JUNE: Mexico?

GRIFFIN: Neutral territory. Acapulco.

JUNE: I've never been to Acapulco.

GRIFFIN: We'll go.

JUNE: Is that the thing to do?

GRIFFIN: It's *a* thing to do.

(*She kisses him.*)

JUNE: Let's do it then.

GRIFFIN: We'll go this weekend.

JUNE: Really? Do I need a passport?
GRIFFIN: Yes.
(*They kiss.*)

EXTERIOR: GRIFFIN'S HOUSE. DAY.
DE LONGPRE *waits outside Griffin's driveway.* GRIFFIN *walks outside and gets in his car. As he pulls out,* DE LONGPRE *flashes* GRIFFIN *his shield.* GRIFFIN *stops.*

DE LONGPRE: Mr. Mill, I'm Detective De Longpre, Pasadena Police.
GRIFFIN: Yes. I recognize you. Did you have a good time at the party last night?
DE LONGPRE: No, I didn't. I'm not supposed to have a good time when I'm on duty,
GRIFFIN: Great. Well, what do you want, Detective De Longpre?
DE LONGPRE: I'd like you to come down to the station.
GRIFFIN: Why?
DE LONGPRE: To look at some pictures.
GRIFFIN: Pictures?
DE LONGPRE: Mug shots. You know, like in the movies.
GRIFFIN: Oh, mug shots, yes, well, all right.
DE LONGPRE: Will you follow me to Pasadena?
GRIFFIN: Pasadena.
DE LONGPRE: Pasadena.
GRIFFIN: Right.
DE LONGPRE: Will you fasten your safety belt, please?

INTERIOR: PASADENA POLICE STATION. DAY.
GRIFFIN *enters the police station.* AVERY *spots him. There is a ruckus between officers and a* MAN *and a* WOMAN *as they walk in.*

MAN: No! Take your hands off of her!
WOMAN: I want my baby!
MAN: Where's her baby at? No!
(*The commotion moves into a back room.*)
AVERY: Mr. Mill.

GRIFFIN: Hello. How are you?

AVERY: Good to see you. Everybody, this is Mr. Mill. You remember. He makes movies. Have a seat, Mr. Mill.

(GRIFFIN *walks directly into the enclosed office.*)

AVERY: Where the fuck is he going? Excuse me, sir, Mr. Mill, Mr. Mill, not in there. That's my lieutenant's office.

(*She leads him to her desk.*)

GRIFFIN: Sorry.

AVERY: Have a seat. Right here. All right, now. (*Referring to a bag on chair.*) Willa, could you? Your desk, thank you. Sorry, have a seat, Mr. Mill. Listen, before we start, Paul rented a movie last night, he came in here raving about. Paul, what was the name of that movie? They changed a lady into a chicken at the end? What did you say?

DE LONGPRE: *Freaks.*

AVERY: *Freaks.* Have you ever seen this?

GRIFFIN: Tod Browning. Yes.

DE LONGPRE (*chanting*): One of us. One of us. One of us.

AVERY: He came in doing that. He was raving about it. He loved it. He loved it. It was thrilling for me. Um, Willa, excuse me, did you happen to see where the tampons went that were in here? (*Looks in desk.*) 'Cause I can't seem to find them.

WILLA: I didn't take them.

AVERY: Who took 'em? (*Referring to* DE LONGPRE:) Did he take them?

WILLA: I don't know. I didn't take them.

AVERY: Well, who did? Damn.

GRIFFIN: Hmm, so, do you have a break in the case?

AVERY: What makes you say that?

GRIFFIN: Why else would you bring me here?

AVERY: Why else indeed? Paul, Paul, why have we brought Mr. Mill in here today?

DE LONGPRE: To look at some pictures.

AVERY: Willa, pictures? Listen, could you, if you remember, what were you wearing that night?

GRIFFIN: I was wearing a double-breasted suit, I believe.

(GRIFFIN *accidentally knocks some files off Avery's desk.* WILLA *picks up the fallen files.*)

AVERY: What's the matter? You're so jumpy, sit down.

GRIFFIN: I'll get it.

AVERY: No, no, that's what she's here for. It's all right, have a seat.

GRIFFIN: Sorry.

(AVERY *opens the file of pictures.*)

AVERY: No problem. Okay. We're going to take a look at this—

(WILLA *places a box of tampons on Avery's desk.*)

AVERY: Where were they? She found them. Look. No, wait a minute, no, no. These aren't mine. These are slender regular, these are yours.

WILLA: Yeah, I guess you have jumbo.

AVERY: Well, I do use jumbo. These are not mine. God, I was trying to help you out. (*To* GRIFFIN:) Look, did you see this guy the night of the murder?

(GRIFFIN *peruses the photos.* DE LONGPRE *swats flies.* GRIFFIN *is growing unnerved.*)

GRIFFIN: Sorry. Hah, no, you're putting me in a terrible position here. I would hate to get the wrong person arrested.

AVERY: Oh, please, this is Pasadena. We do not arrest the wrong person. That's L.A. You see L.A., they kick your ass, then they arrest you. That's what they do. We don't do that. Remember last year—what was that guy's name?—they put him on the tape. What was that?

WILLA: King.

AVERY: That's right, King. Now *he* was the wrong guy.

GRIFFIN: Do you have a witness?

AVERY: I can't answer that.

GRIFFIN: Either you have a witness, or these are suspects in similar murders.

AVERY: Mr. Mill, have you been going to detective school?

GRIFFIN: No, actually, we're doing a movie right now called *The Lonely Room,* and Scott Glenn plays a detective much like yourself.

AVERY: He plays a black woman?

GRIFFIN: No.

WILLA: Oh, Lily Tomlin's in that. I read about that. I like her.

GRIFFIN: Actually, I was making the comparison not based on race or gender.

AVERY: Speaking of which, did you go out with June . . . *(To* DE LONGPRE:*)* What's that woman's name?

DE LONGPRE: Gudmundsdottir.

AVERY: What is it? Spell it for me.

DE LONGPRE *(sixty miles per hour)*: *G-u-d-m-u-n-d-s-d-o-t-t-i-r.*

AVERY: Oh, that really helps. Did you go out with June . . .

GRIFFIN: Gudmundsdottir—

AVERY: Yeah, her. Last night—

GRIFFIN: Yes, I did.

AVERY: Have you guys known each other a long time?

GRIFFIN: No. I spoke to her for the first time the night Kahane was killed.

AVERY: Wow, so you didn't know her before this?

GRIFFIN: No. We met over the phone. We got to talking, and one thing led to another.

AVERY: Did you fuck her?

GRIFFIN: What kind of question is that?

AVERY: I think it's pretty direct. Did. You. Fuck. Her?

GRIFFIN: Well, I wouldn't answer that question without a lawyer in the room. And *then* I probably wouldn't even answer that question. Why don't you ask your friend here? He's been following me all over the place. He'll probably know.

AVERY *(to* DE LONGPRE*)*: All right. Paul, did Mr. Mill fuck June Guntmnhertrn?

DE LONGPRE: I didn't see him.

AVERY: Well, see you got away with it.

(GRIFFIN *begins to unravel*.)

GRIFFIN: What are you implying?

AVERY: I'm not implying anything. I asked you a direct question: Did you fuck her?

GRIFFIN: And I told you, I wouldn't answer that question without a lawyer in the room.

AVERY: Then why are you getting hot under the collar?

GRIFFIN: Because you're being rude, Ms. Avery.

AVERY: Oh, well, excuse me. I think it's kind of soon for her to be gallivanting in the streets with you.

GRIFFIN: I'm there for her as a friend, Ms. Avery.

AVERY: Hmmm.

GRIFFIN: Why don't you call her? I'm sure she would be happy to pick over the horror of what's happened and tell you how we became friends. What is this, fucking Iran? Since when does the state tell us how long and with whom we can share our grief?

(AVERY *starts to laugh.*

She continues laughing.

Soon, everybody's laughing. GRIFFIN *unravels*.)

GRIFFIN: Are you holding June (*fumbling his words*) Gudmundsdottir to some special code of conduct reserved for women? What the fuck are you laughing at? (*Standing*.) I'd like to talk to my lawyer.

(*Everyone is laughing hard.*)

DE LONGPRE (*chanting*): One of us . . . One of us . . .

INTERIOR: GRIFFIN'S OFFICE. DAY.

WALTER *is in the office.* GRIFFIN *lies on the couch.*

WALTER: It's time for you to get yourself a real good lawyer.

GRIFFIN: I had a drink with the guy, Walter, that's all.

WALTER: If you went to Pasadena with intent to kill, you could go to the gas chamber.

GRIFFIN: I went to Pasadena with the intent to hire.

WALTER: So you say.

(JAN *comes into the office.*)

JAN: Griffin, the Schecter brothers are here.

(*The two* SCHECTER *brothers,* CARL *and* ERIC, *manic film-school gradu-ates, in love with their bad reputations, invade the office.*)

ERIC SCHECTER: Griffin, Griffin, Griffin. Don't make us wait.

CARL SCHECTER (*indicates* WALTER): Who is this man?

ERIC SCHECTER: Oh, and the travel agent called. You're confirmed.

JAN: He grabbed the phone from me.

WALTER: Travel agent?

GRIFFIN: I'm going to Puerto Vallarta tomorrow.

WALTER: You're leaving the country?

GRIFFIN: For the weekend.

(*The* SCHECTERS *watch this like a tennis match.*)

WALTER: That's a risk.

JAN: Why?

GRIFFIN: Because Larry Levy could have my office in three days. That's what Walter thinks.

JAN (*panicked about her job*): You know something I don't know?

WALTER: You're pretty smooth.

GRIFFIN: I sleep at night.

WALTER: You really should run a studio.

GRIFFIN: Tell a friend.

(WALTER *leaves. He passes the gauntlet.*

As soon as WALTER *is gone:*)

ERIC SCHECTER: Yeah, Walter, it's been real. Griffin, we're tired of shopping everything around. We want to go ex-clusive, one studio. Carl, how much have our last three pictures made?

CARL SCHECTER: A hundred and five million dollars.

(GRIFFIN *isn't listening.*)

ERIC SCHECTER: That's not a lot. I know some people do better, but we're consistent, and we're always under budget.

CARL SCHECTER: Forget it, Eric, he's not listening. Let's go to Columbia.

ERIC SCHECTER: We already went to Columbia.

CARL SCHECTER: Oh yeah. What did they say?

(BONNIE *pokes her head into the office.*)

GRIFFIN (*panicked, contains it, and annoyed by the brothers' routine*): Bonnie.

THE SCHECTERS: Hey, Bon.

BONNIE: I got the Tom Wolfe book.

GRIFFIN: Congratulations.

CARL SCHECTER: Bonnie, make him give us a deal. We want a home.

ERIC SCHECTER: We're tired of shopping everything around.

BONNIE: Really? I thought that's how you guys like to do business.

CARL SCHECTER: We've changed our minds.

GRIFFIN (*to* BONNIE): I'll talk to you later.

BONNIE: Levison said you're going out of town tomorrow.

GRIFFIN: For the weekend.

BONNIE: Are you going with someone named June something?

GRIFFIN: Yes.

BONNIE: You took her to a party, Griffin, with several hundred of my best friends.

GRIFFIN: She's recently widowed. You weren't in town. So I took her.

BONNIE: And now you're taking her to Mexico for the weekend.

ERIC SCHECTER: Carl, let's get out of here. Mom and Dad are fighting.

GRIFFIN: Guys, have your lawyer give me a call. You've got a deal.

CARL SCHECTER: Yes!

ERIC SCHECTER: Carl, let's get out of here before he changes his mind.

CARL SCHECTER: We have a witness.

(BONNIE *knows her affair with* GRIFFIN *is over.*)
BONNIE: Have a good trip.

EXTERIOR: AIRPORT. DAY.

GRIFFIN *drives up with* JUNE. *He parks at the curb and gets out. He goes to the trunk and opens it.* JUNE *gets out and starts to join him.* GRIFFIN *looks toward the entrance and sees* DE LONGPRE *talking to a policeman. The camera zooms in.* GRIFFIN *turns to* JUNE.

GRIFFIN: Uhh, did you bring your passport?

JUNE: Yes.

GRIFFIN: Do you want to hear something funny? I forgot mine.

JUNE: Ohh. Does that mean we have to go back and get it? Will we miss the plane?

(GRIFFIN *closes the door on her and gets in the car on his side.*)

GRIFFIN: It's so stupid of me. We'll never make another plane today. Damn it! Well, it's all right. Anyway, I've got a better idea. Do you like the desert?

JUNE: I've never been to the desert. Why?

GRIFFIN: You've never been in the desert? I know of a great hideaway in Desert Hot Springs. We'll go there. It's a two-hour drive. I know the people; we'll call ahead.

JUNE: Are we hiding?

GRIFFIN: Yeah, we're hiding, we're hiding from everybody. You'll like it there. It'll probably remind you of Iceland.

(*He drives out.*)

EXTERIOR: GRIFFIN'S CAR. DUSK.

As the car drives through the desert, it passes windmills, a snake in the rocks, and arrives at Two Bunch Palms.

EXTERIOR: TWO BUNCH PALMS. DUSK.

As Griffin's car drives through the security gate:

GUARD: Evening, Mr. M. You're all checked in. The Capone building, you know where it is . . .

GRIFFIN: Yes. Thank you, Walter.

(*He drives in. The* GUARD *picks up a telephone.*)

EXTERIOR: OUTSIDE DINING AREA. NIGHT.

A pig roasts on a spit. GRIFFIN *and* JUNE *enter the area and go to a table. There is a champagne bucket at the table. Almost no one is around. Music is playing. He seats her. She looks around and whispers to him.*

JUNE: Hey, look, the water looks like it's steaming.

GRIFFIN: It comes out of the ground that way.

JUNE: There not many people around?

GRIFFIN: Well, they're fully booked, actually. Fifty rooms, a hundred people.

JUNE: Where are they all?

GRIFFIN: Hiding.

(*A* WAITER *suddenly appears and opens the champagne.*)

WAITER: Sir?

GRIFFIN: A couple of Banning Springs Waters, please.

WAITER: Right away, Mr. M.

JUNE: Do places like this really exist?

GRIFFIN: Only in the movies.

(*A naked couple across from them glides into the hot springs.*)

EXTERIOR: DINING AREA. NIGHT.

GRIFFIN *and* JUNE *are dancing.*

JUNE: Tell me about the movies you make.

GRIFFIN: Why?

JUNE: Because I want to know what you do.

GRIFFIN: Well, I listen to stories and decide if they'll make good movies or not. I get 125 phone calls a day, and if I let that slip to a hundred, I know that I'm not doing my job.

(GRIFFIN *and* JUNE *walk down to the edge of the spa.*)

GRIFFIN: And when they call, they want to know one thing: they want me to say yes to them and make their movie. If I say yes to them and make their movie, they think come New Year's, it's going to be them and Jack Nicholson on the slopes of Aspen, that's what they think. The problem is, I can only say yes—my studio can only say yes—twelve times a year. Collectively, we hear about fifty thousand stories a year, so it's hard; and I guess sometimes I'm not nice and make enemies. And that's what I was to David, an enemy.

JUNE: Was his story one of the twelve?

GRIFFIN: No, it wasn't.

JUNE: Why?

GRIFFIN: It lacked certain elements that we need to market a film successfully.

JUNE: What elements?

GRIFFIN: Suspense, laughter, violence, hope, heart, nudity, sex, happy endings. Mainly happy endings.

JUNE: What about reality?

GRIFFIN: You're not from Iceland, are you?

JUNE: Did I say that? Hmmm. Why don't you put me in the hot springs and see if I melt.

INTERIOR: CAPONE CABIN. NIGHT.

GRIFFIN *and* JUNE *are in bed, making love. They glide into each other's sweat.* GRIFFIN *is desperate to confess.*

GRIFFIN: I love you.

JUNE: I know that.

GRIFFIN: There's something you don't know. Something I have to tell you.

JUNE: Be careful.

GRIFFIN: June. David's death . . .

JUNE: Don't, don't, not tonight . . .

GRIFFIN: . . . Please, there's something you have to know . . .

JUNE: Shhh. Don't say anything more.

GRIFFIN: Baby, I was responsible.

JUNE: I love you, don't . . .

GRIFFIN: It was my fault.

JUNE: Don't. Don't. Oh . . .

(*It is too much for both of them.*)

EXTERIOR: SPA. DAY.

GRIFFIN *and* JUNE *are side by side in mud baths, covered in mud. They are both staring at the sky. Their expressions reveal nothing. A* MAS-SEUR *comes in.*

MASSEUR: Mr. M, Mr. M, sorry to disturb you, there's a telephone call, and it sounds important.

GRIFFIN (*from the mud*): Who is it?

MASSEUR: A Mr. Dick Mellen. He says he's your lawyer.

(GRIFFIN *climbs out of the mud, dripping mud. He goes to the phone, a sight.*)

GRIFFIN: Dick? How'd you find me?

MELLEN (*voice-over*): Come on, Griff. Who the hell do you think you're talking to?

GRIFFIN: Yeah, what's going on?

EXTERIOR: MELLEN'S HOUSE. DAY.

MELLEN *is on the phone.*

MELLEN: Levison's out.

GRIFFIN: Out?

MELLEN: They gave him six hours to clean out his office.

GRIFFIN: Who's taking over?

MELLEN: Nothing's been decided. All we know for sure is that Reggie Goldman went home with the clap or something.

GRIFFIN: Well, am I in a position to—

MELLEN: Listen, I don't want to talk about studio politics. Why the hell didn't you tell me about this Kahane business?

GRIFFIN: Kahane, I tried to, Dick.

MELLEN: You didn't try hard enough. You better be at the Pasadena Police station in about four hours.

GRIFFIN: Pasadena? What for?

MELLEN: For a fucking line-up, that's what for. They got a witness, evidently. Now, look, I found you a guy; his name is Gar Girard. He's a top-flight criminal lawyer. He's tough. He's hard-nosed. Don't you talk to anybody else. Just get there.

GRIFFIN: I'll be there.

MELLEN: Griffin, this is a tough one. Good luck. (MELLEN *hangs up.*)

GRIFFIN: Thanks.

INTERIOR: POLICE STATION. DAY.

GRIFFIN *comes into the station followed by* DE LONGPRE. AVERY *and* WALTER *get up to greet him.*

WALTER: Mr. Mill. The studio's very upset about the publicity this might, uhh, generate. But I'll handle the press, the police, the judge, and the witness, if I can.

AVERY: Mr. Mill, thanks for coming down without a fight. You know it's really in your best interest.

(GARFIELD GIRARD *rolls into the lobby. He is in a wheelchair, wearing a Reebok jacket. He's in his midthirties, energetic, focused.*)

GIRARD: Mr. Mill, get away from that woman, she's the enemy. Hi, Susan, I had a lovely time at the Met the other night.

AVERY: I can't believe you remembered.

(*As* GIRARD *talks, they move through the police station to the line-up rooms.*)

GIRARD (*to* GRIFFIN): Mr. Mill, Gar Girard, I'm here to represent you. Dick Mellen called me in on this. Here's the situation. They got a witness, and they want you to do a line-up. Now, if you say *no* they'll arrest you, I'm certain of that. And even if you get identified, I'll get you out on bail. Now, this witness lives across the street from the parking lot. Even if she makes an identification, a posi-

tive ID right now, even if that happens—it was very late
at night—by the time I'm finished with her, the world will
have a new legal standard for blindness. Keep the faith,
we'll do what we can.

(AVERY *points* GRIFFIN *to the line-up room.*)

INTERIOR: LINE-UP ROOM. DAY.

AVERY, MRS. BUNNY *from the Rialto,* GIRARD, WILLA, *and a* LINE-UP
OFFICER *are in the room. Through the one-way glass, we see* GRIF-
FIN *standing in front of a height graph painted on the wall. There
are six men in the line-up, three of them vaguely Griffin's size
and shape. Number 3 is* DE LONGPRE. *They look at their reflec-
tions, and* GRIFFIN *tries to see beyond. Impossible.* GRIFFIN *is num-
ber 5.*

WILLA: You don't have to worry about a thing. You can
see them, but they can't see you. Just tell the truth.

MRS. BUNNY: Because I saw him—

AVERY: All right, fire it up.

LINE-UP OFFICER (*into intercom*): Number One, step for-
ward . . . make a quarter turn to the right . . . face for-
ward . . . (*Continues.*)

GIRARD: Are those prescription glasses, Mrs. Bunny?

AVERY: You can't ask her that.

GIRARD: Sorry.

MRS. BUNNY: It's very hard, you know.

AVERY: Oh yeah. I know.

GIRARD: Take your time.

(MRS. BUNNY *is very nervous and strains to look through her glasses.*)

MRS. BUNNY: You don't want to pick the wrong one.

AVERY: No. God forbid.

WILLA: Now, you just take your time.

AVERY: Anybody look vaguely familiar?

MRS. BUNNY: . . . No, I . . .

AVERY: Take your time.

LINE-UP OFFICER: . . . Step back into position, Number
Three, take one step forward . . .

MRS. BUNNY: This is not easy . . .

AVERY: I know it isn't.

GIRARD: It never is, Mrs. Bunny.

MRS. BUNNY: I mean, I am trying.

AVERY/GIRARD (*at once*): Yes. Take your time.

MRS. BUNNY: And I did see him clearly . . . uhhh . . . no, no, I don't—

AVERY: Look real hard. Take a good look.

MRS. BUNNY: I did, I did. I am. Hmm, could I see . . . umm . . . Number Three again.

LINE-UP OFFICER: Call Number Three.

AVERY: Wait a minute, wait a minute, Simone.

MRS. BUNNY: Could I see . . .

GIRARD: Did she call the wrong number—

LINE-UP OFFICER: . . . Leave your hat off, Number Four . . .

AVERY: Excuse me. Excuse me.

GIRARD: If she wants to see him again, thank you—

LINE-UP OFFICER: . . . Number Five, could you take one step forward?

(GRIFFIN *turns. We see his profile. A dangerous moment.*)

AVERY: Which number?

MRS. BUNNY: Excuse me.

AVERY: Number Five . . .

GIRARD: Susan, I think she can call who she's interested in.

AVERY: You're absolutely right.

MRS. BUNNY: No, no, the other one. That one.

AVERY: Which one?

GIRARD: By the *number.*

(*The camera zooms in on* DE LONGPRE.)

MRS. BUNNY: Oh, hmm, it's not Number Six.

GIRARD: Not Number Six.

AVERY: What about Number Five?

MRS. BUNNY: Three.

GIRARD: Three.

LINE-UP OFFICER: Step forward, Number Three.

AVERY: What do you mean "Number Three"?

GIRARD: I think she can request who she wants to see.

AVERY: Just a second, just a second.

GIRARD: Just a second? She wants to see Number Three.

(AVERY *turns to* MRS. BUNNY. *The witness points.*)

MRS. BUNNY: Him. That's him. I'd swear on my mother's grave.

GIRARD: Number Three. I think we're concluded here today, Ms. Avery.

MRS. BUNNY: Number Three.

GIRARD: Number Three.

AVERY: Number Three.

GIRARD: We heard what she said.

AVERY: Yes, I would say so.

LINE-UP OFFICER: Okay, Doug, take him out.

GIRARD: Number Three, thank you.

AVERY (*to* MRS. BUNNY): Ma'am, may I be personal? Where the fuck is your mother buried?

(GIRARD *laughs.*)

AVERY: Everybody, let's get out of here.

GIRARD: Let's get out of this sauna.

AVERY: Out.

EXTERIOR: POLICE STATION. DAY.

GRIFFIN, WALTER, *and* GIRARD *come out of the police station and pause on the entrance steps.*

GIRARD: I don't know who got to that witness, but she sure wrapped up my case—picking that cop. You're a lucky man, Mr. Mill. (*Sees his predicament.*) Goddamn it, no ramp again.

WALTER: Witnesses can't be relied on. Remember *Witness for the Prosecution?* Marlene Dietrich and Tyrone Power?

GIRARD: That's it, you're as free as a bird . . . No witnesss—no crime.

WALTER: That Avery woman thinks you just got away with murder—

GIRARD: Everybody does, Mr. Mill.

(GRIFFIN *walks away.*

AVERY, DE LONGPRE, *and* WILLA *watch from a second-floor window.*)

TITLE CARD: —ONE YEAR LATER—

INTERIOR: GAS CHAMBER. NIGHT.
From the prisoner's point of view: preparations for an execution. Among the witnesses are PETER FALK *and* SUSAN SARANDON. RAY WALSTON, *as the chaplain, whispers the last rites. We move through the bars of a cell, and we see the prisoner is* JULIA ROBERTS.
The executioner prepares the cyanide pellets. The prisoner is led from her cell into the chamber. The guards strap the prisoner in: arms, legs, chest.

INTERIOR: SCREENING ROOM. DAY.
We pull back and see the crew, OAKLEY, CIVELLA, GRIFFIN, MARTY, LEVY, *and* BONNIE *watching the film.*
ON-SCREEN.
The chaplain makes the sign of the cross in front of the prisoner. The guards and the chaplain leave the chamber. Chilling. There is an awful sound of the door being screwed shut.
The pellets are released into the acid bath under the chair.
Prisoner's point of view: the witnesses watch her die. The sound of the prisoner's final, rasping breaths.
SCREENING ROOM.
> WHITNEY (*whispers to* LEVY): You have made a wonderful
> movie. It's perfect. It's Oscar time, Larry.
ON-SCREEN.
The blinds on the chamber are closed. We cut to a GUARD *on the telephone.*
> GUARD: What!?
OUTSIDE THE CHAMBER.
We see what they see: running down the hall, looking crazed, is BRUCE WILLIS.

BRUCE WILLIS: It's too late, come on!

(*He grabs a shotgun out of a guard's hand and points it at the chamber window. He blasts the window of the gas chamber.*)

BRUCE WILLIS: Stand back!

(JULIA ROBERTS *is barely conscious, and* BRUCE WILLIS *is at her side. He carries her out past the witnesses, who begin to applaud. The music swells.*)

JULIA ROBERTS: What took you so long?

BRUCE WILLIS: Traffic was a bitch.

INTERIOR: SCREENING ROOM. DAY.

We pull back from the screen. LEVY *stands up, applauding. We see the crew,* OAKLEY, CIVELLA, *and* BONNIE.

LEVY: It's outstanding. The audience is going to love it.

BONNIE: You sold it out, I can't believe it, how could you let him sell it out? What about the truth? What about reality?

OAKLEY: What about the way the old ending tested in Canoga Park? Everybody hated it. We reshot it. Now everybody loves it. That's *reality*.

BONNIE: But you had an ending which was true! You didn't give it a chance.

CIVELLA: Larry, who is this person? Doesn't she know about working with grown-ups?

LEVY: Bonnie . . . goddamn it, goddamn it, this is a hit! This is what we are here for.

BONNIE: Yeah, well, it didn't have to end this way!

LEVY: I want you out of here.

CIVELLA: Good thinking, Larry.

BONNIE: I'm going over your head, Larry.

LEVY: Bonnie, you're fired.

BONNIE: Fuck you.

LEVY: Oh, it takes more to make it in this business than a dirty mouth.

MARTY: Gentlemen, the campaign.

(*He shows off the poster.*)

* * *

EXTERIOR: STUDIO. DAY.
BONNIE *charges across the lot toward Levison's bungalow. Her heel collapses, and she falls. She gets up, limping across the lot.*

INTERIOR: LEVISON'S BUNGALOW. DAY.
GRIFFIN *sits in Levison's old chair. He runs the studio. We don't take much time to register the news. He plays executive basketball with* WALTER.

INTERIOR: LEVISON'S RECEPTION ROOM. DAY.
FRANK, *a studio executive we saw early on, has just come out of the inner office.* BONNIE *enters the reception room in tears.* CELIA *tries to put her off.*

> BONNIE: Celia, it's very important. I need to talk to him now.
> CELIA: No, Bonnie, he's very busy.
> BONNIE: Celia, please, it's me, Bonnie. We're friends.
> CELIA: Bonnie, don't you understand, I'm not just me, I am also the job.
> BONNIE: Please. Please. Please.
> CELIA: Honey, all right, I'll try.

(CELIA *goes into the office.*)

> BASKETBALL: Three points! Take that!
> CELIA: Oh, Walter, stop that nonsense. Griffin, it's Bonnie. She's here.
> GRIFFIN: Did Levy fire her?
> CELIA: Yes, sir, I guess he did.
> GRIFFIN: Well, I can't see her now. I promised I'd be home early. Tell her I'll get back to her. Walter, get your foot off the fuckin' couch.
> CELIA: Tell her yourself.

(GRIFFIN *takes a deep breath, stands up, and walks out of the office.*)

* * *

INTERIOR: LEVISON'S OUTER OFFICE. DAY.

GRIFFIN *passes through.* BONNIE *is sitting there in tears.* JAN *is answering the phone.*

SANDY: Griffin, it's Larry Levy's office—it's very important

(GRIFFIN *is on his way out the door. He pays no special attention to* BONNIE.)

BONNIE: Griffin, Griffin, Griffin, I have to talk to you. Griffin, please. Griffin, please can we talk about it.

(*He is going out the door.* CELIA *and* BONNIE *follow him.*)

GRIFFIN: Bonnie . . . you'll land on your feet. I know it. You're a survivor.

(JIMMY *pulls up with Griffin's car—a convertible Rolls-Royce.*)

CELIA: Griffin, it's Larry Levy's office. He says it's very important.

GRIFFIN: Give it a minute, transfer to the car phone.

(BONNIE *sits on the stairs. She is crying. As soon as he gets in the car,* CELIA *transfers the call.*)

EXTERIOR: STREET. DAY.

Griffin's Rolls-Royce drives along. The phone rings, and he answers it.

GRIFFIN: Yeah.

SANDY (*on phone*): Griffin, I have Larry Levy on the line.

GRIFFIN: Larry, how'd the screening go? How's my new ending?

LEVY (*voice-over*): Fantastic, fantastic. Worked like gangbusters. That's why you get the big bucks, Griff.

GRIFFIN: Yeah, yeah, yeah, stop kissing my ass, Larry. What do you want? Can't this wait?

LEVY (*voice-over*): I don't think it should. This is hot. I've got a writer in here who's got a pitch I think you ought to hear. I think it's something we should go for. It's a great idea.

GRIFFIN: Yeah, who's the writer?

LEVY (*voice-over*): I'll put him on the speaker. Hold on a minute.

WRITER (*voice-over*): Hiya, Griff. Remember me? I'm the asshole who used to be in the postcard business.

(*It is the* POSTCARD WRITER. *We know his voice.*)

GRIFFIN: You!

WRITER (*voice-over*): That's right. The king of suspense himself. You remember me.

GRIFFIN: I haven't heard from you for a while . . .

WRITER (*voice-over*): Well, I've been busy. I've been writing a script. I got inspired.

LEVY (*voice-over*): Okay, tell him. Give him the pitch. You're going to love this, Griffin. It's great.

WRITER (*voice-over*): All right, it's a Hollywood story, Griff, a real thriller.

(*We move in on* GRIFFIN *as he drives in a residential neighborhood until we are close.*)

WRITER (*voice-over*): It's about a shitbag producer, a studio exec, who murders a writer he thinks is harassing him. Problem is he kills the wrong writer. Now he's got to deal with blackmail as well as the cops. But here's the switch. Son of a bitch, he gets away with it.

GRIFFIN: Larry? Get off the speaker. I want to talk to him privately.

LEVY (*voice-over*): Sure thing. It's a winner, Griffin, it's a winner . . .

(*We hear the speaker go off, and* GRIFFIN *is now alone on the line with the* WRITER.)

GRIFFIN: Gets away with it?

WRITER (*voice-over*): Absolutely, it's a Hollywood ending, Griff. He marries the dead writer's girl, and they live happily ever after.

GRIFFIN: You guarantee that ending?

WRITER (*voice-over*): If the price is right, you got it.

GRIFFIN: If you can guarantee me that ending, you got a deal.

WRITER (*voice-over*): I guarantee it, Griff.

GRIFFIN: What do you call this thing, anyway?

WRITER (*voice-over*): *The Player.*

GRIFFIN (*turns it over, it fits*): *The Player?* . . . I like that.

(*He hangs up.*)

EXTERIOR: GRIFFIN'S NEW HOUSE. DAY.

GRIFFIN *pulls into the driveway of his Brentwood estate, a garden of flowers, the perfect house.* JUNE, *eight months pregnant, comes out the front door to meet him as he gets out of the Rolls-Royce.*

JUNE: What took you so long?

GRIFFIN: Traffic was a bitch.

(*They kiss. Music takes over.*)

The Rapture

Filmmakers

Director and Writer	Michael Tolkin
Executive Producer	Laurie Parker
Producer	Nick Wechsler
Producer	Nancy Tenenbaum
Producer	Karen Koch
Director of Photography	Bojan Bazelli
Editor	Suzanne Fenn
Production Designer	Robin Standefer
Music	Thomas Newman
Casting	Deborah Aquila

Cast

Sharon	Mimi Rogers
Randy	David Duchovny
Vic	Patrick Bauchau
Mary	Kimberly Cullum
Sheriff Foster	Will Patton
Paula	Terri Hanauer
Henry	Dick Anthony Williams
Tommy	James Le Gros
Angie	Carole Davis
The First Boy	De Vaughn Nixon
The Older Boy	Christian Belnavis
Louis	Douglas Roberts
1st Evangelist	Scott Burkholder
2nd Evangelist	Vince Grant
Diana	Stephanie Menuez
Maggie	Darwin Carson
Executive	Patrick Dollaghan
Bartender	Marvin Elkins
Wayne	Sam Vlahos
Conrad	Rustam Branaman
Rock Climber	Denney Pierce
Cashier	Joshua Farrell
Manager	Andrew Pressman
Guard	Kerry Leigh Michaels
Angels	Henry Kingi, Linda Albertano
Man on Television	Michael David Lally

INTERIOR: TELEPHONE COMPANY INFORMATION OFFICE. DAY.
We move slowly through a crowded office. A hundred information operators in booths. SHARON *works at a computer terminal. Close on her. She's on a kind of autopilot as she does her job, and the people talking to her hear so little personality that her humanity barely registers. That she might have a beauty that is becoming hollow, or a private life that would astonish them—this, no one thinks about. She watches the clock. Five minutes to six.*

SHARON: Please hold for the number. Operator 134, what city please? (*Pause, as she types in the name.*) Is that a business or residence? Please hold for the number. (*Pause.*) Operator 134. What city please? (*Pause.*) How do you spell that?

(*The clock. Two minutes to six.*)

SHARON (*pause*): Please hold for the number. (*Pause.*) Operator 134. What city please? (*Pause.*) Is that a business or residence? (*Pause.*) Please hold for the number.

(*Pause. Behind her, a woman, another* OPERATOR, *waits for the chair.*

Six o'clock.

SHARON *gets up. The other* OPERATOR *takes her place and takes her headphones.* SHARON *starts to stand as she begins the next sentence. Pause.*)

SHARON: *Operator 134. Is that a business or residence?* . . .

(*And the other* OPERATOR *takes her headset and completes the number as* SHARON *leaves her post.*)

OPERATOR: Please hold for the number.

(SHARON *walks away.*

Cut to:)

* * *

EXTERIOR: STREET. NIGHT.

And now we see her sitting in the back of a Jaguar convertible. VIC *is driving the car.* VIC *looks to someone offscreen.*

VIC: What about them?

SHARON: No. He's wearing a rug, and she has a nose job.

VIC: It's not a bad nose job.

SHARON: They're all bad.

(*Now we see* VIC. *He is a beardless werewolf* [I mean, spiritually]. SHARON *is excited. She likes danger. Underneath, we feel her deep exhaustion.*)

SHARON: Let's go to the Continental Club.

VIC: Really?

SHARON: Come on, Vic, you don't want to go back to the airport.

(*He's thinking.*)

VIC: I like the airport. I like the bars at the airport hotels. I like tourists. (*Meaning the bar:*) I don't want that tonight.

SHARON: What's the matter, are you scared of getting dirty?

VIC (*uncertain*): Maybe.

SHARON: C'mon, Vic. That's the place to start. Let's have some fun.

(*From her challenging smile, his laugh, we cut to:*)

INTERIOR: BAR. NIGHT.

A rummy's bar in Hollywood. SHARON *and* VIC *lean against a wall, drinking from bottles.* VIC *studies a couple sitting alone at a table, side by side. Sharp-featured, long-haired, not talking, they are smoking.*

SHARON: I like them.

VIC: You would.

(SHARON *and* VIC *walk across the floor to the table. They slide into the seat facing the couple. Call her* DIANA. *Call him* RANDY.)

VIC: I'm Vic.

SHARON: I'm Sharon.

VIC: Hi.

(RANDY *and* DIANA *are quietly amused.*)

 RANDY: What brings you to this side of town?

 SHARON: We got tired of shooting the dogs where the rich people live.

 DIANA: What are you looking for now?

 SHARON: Now we're looking for something a little less obvious.

 VIC: But fun. Definitely fun. We're very social people.

 RANDY: You might be asking for something you couldn't handle.

 SHARON: I can handle it.

 RANDY: What if things go out of control?

 SHARON: What's control got to do with it?

 VIC: I think he wants to find out if you have any limits.

 SHARON: Tell him that I haven't found them yet.

 VIC: Sharon hasn't found her limits yet.

 DIANA: Talk, talk, talk. (*To* RANDY:) Let's go somewhere.

 VIC: I have a store. Let's go to the store.

(*They stand up.* VIC *takes Diana's hand.* RANDY *and* SHARON *follow. Cut to:*)

INTERIOR: VIC'S STORE. NIGHT.

VIC *leads the others in, turning on lights and slow dance music (Little Richard singing "Directly from My Heart"). We move through the store to a far corner, to a model bedroom.*

SHARON *reaches out to* RANDY *and pulls him to her.* RANDY *lets go of* DIANA *and dances with* SHARON. *They dance to be watched. They are moving toward a bed.* DIANA *takes Vic's hand. They dance. A blues song plays.*

 RANDY: Come here. Come here and have a seat.

 SHARON: Come on, let's fool around.

(RANDY *lifts* SHARON *into his arms.*)

 SHARON: Ohh. What a man.

 RANDY: Nice store you got here, Vic. Nice.

(SHARON *dances slowly with* RANDY; *they grind into each other, putting on a show.* SHARON *and* VIC *watch each other.*)

DIANA: Come on. Show me what you mean by fun.

VIC: Unnh-uhh.

(SHARON *sees this and shakes her head.* DIANA *goes to* RANDY *and* SHARON.)

SHARON: Vic likes to watch.

RANDY: Watch this.

(*And we stay with Vic's face as the other three fall on the bed. Dissolve to:*)

INTERIOR: VIC'S STORE. NIGHT.

SHARON, RANDY, *and* DIANA *on a bed. Their sex is a ritual, and the surprise here is their need.* SHARON *is the subject. They finish. They are still for a moment.* SHARON *gets up. We watch* RANDY *watching her.*

SHARON *sits on the arm of a leather couch, smoking.* RANDY *comes over to her. Behind them,* VIC *begins fucking* DIANA. SHARON *looks grim.* RANDY *studies her.*

RANDY: Was that far enough?

(SHARON *turns to look at him.*)

SHARON: Randy, right?

RANDY: Hey, you remembered my name.

SHARON: Hi, Randy.

RANDY: Was it enough?

SHARON: That was . . . interesting.

(*The camera pulls back. We hear* DIANA *as* VIC *tries to come. Cut to:*)

INTERIOR: TELEPHONE COMPANY INFORMATION OFFICE. DAY.

SHARON *works at a computer terminal. Close on her.*

SHARON: Operator 134, what city please? (*Pause, as she types in the name.*) Is that a business or residence? (*Pause.*) Hold for the number. (*Pause.*) This is operator

134. What city? (*Pause.*) Can you spell that? (*Pause.*) Is
that *D* as in *Dick?* (*Pause.*) Please hold for the number.
(*Cut to:*)

INTERIOR: TELEPHONE COMPANY VENDING-MACHINE ROOM. DAY.
*Coffee break. Move through the room. Everyone sits alone, recovering
from the phones.* SHARON *enters staring into space. Behind her are a
group of workers, talking quietly but passionately. At first,* SHARON
doesn't listen. Bits of the following drift into consciousness.

WORKER #1: Hi, Wayne. It was much stronger last night,
wasn't it?

WORKER #2: By a factor of five.

WORKER #3: It was almost like the first time, I mean, it was
that clear.

WORKER #1: And the horn, the sound of a horn, that was
new.

WORKER #2: One note, a very clear tone. I found it on my
piano; it's B flat.

WORKER #1: What do you think?

(SHARON *has leaned back in her chair to eavesdrop.*)

WORKER #3: I think it's going to happen, and soon. Have
you been praying?

(WORKER #2, *facing Sharon's back, sees her leaning in and puts a
finger to his lips.*)

WORKER #2: Yes, as much as I can.

(*The other two glance over their shoulders at* SHARON. *She looks over
her shoulder and sees them look at her. She pulls her chair forward.*)

WORKER #3: What does The Boy say?

WORKER #1: Not yet.

(*Cut to:*)

INTERIOR: SHARON'S APARTMENT. NIGHT.
She is in bed with RANDY. *Under the sheet, he strokes her. She comes,
pushing his hand away.*

SHARON: Tell me a story.

RANDY: Hmmm.

(*He tries to start again.*)

SHARON: No, no, no. I already know that story. Tell me something new.

(*He thinks about it.*)

RANDY: I've done things for money.

SHARON: Like what?

RANDY: Things I wish I hadn't.

SHARON: Like what?

RANDY: I killed a man once.

SHARON: For how much?

RANDY: For a thousand dollars.

SHARON: That's not very much money.

RANDY: It was a lot then. All I can say now is, I wish I hadn't.

SHARON: Why?

RANDY: 'Cause it stays with me. I mean, I killed a man. I took his life, his only life. That's bad.

SHARON: Did you know him?

RANDY: No.

SHARON: Well, why did the people who paid you want him dead?

RANDY: There are some questions you don't ask. After that, they offered me another job, the same kind of job, better money.

SHARON: And did you do it?

RANDY: No. But I think about that killing a lot. I think, you know, if we weren't taught that killing is bad, would I still feel as bad?

SHARON: I don't know.

RANDY: You don't know. Are you scared of me now?

SHARON: Did anyone pay you to kill me?

(*A long pause.*)

RANDY: That was not a good year. 1975, that was my best year. I was nineteen. What was your best year?

SHARON: Hmmm. I guess I'm still waiting. I don't know. I

don't know. Everything just seems so empty. Time passes
so quickly.

RANDY: Yeah? I think it's kind of slow.

SHARON: No, I mean, like a day. You know, a day is
always just over . . . I don't know what I'm trying to say.

RANDY: I think I understand.

SHARON: Oh really? Why don't you let me in on my secret.

RANDY: I think that you are depressed, and I think that
you should see a therapist.

SHARON: Oh, that's great. That's fucking brilliant.

(*Cut to:*)

INTERIOR: SHARON'S APARTMENT. DAY.

SHARON *pulls subscription cards out of magazines. A door bell rings;
then there's a knock at the door.* SHARON *answers it. Two men wear-
ing suits, white shirts, and dark ties are there.*

*Both are in their late thirties or early forties. In New York, you would
assume they were bankers or painters trying to look like bankers.
They are evangelists. None of the evangelists in this film sound like
TV preachers or have a hint of the South in their accents.*

FIRST EVANGELIST: You understand that these are the last
days. It can't go on like this. God is coming back. His
prophecies are now being fulfilled.

SECOND EVANGELIST: You have to accept Jesus as your Lord
and Savior.

SHARON: Otherwise . . .

FIRST EVANGELIST: You won't be saved.

(*She shuts the door. Pause. She opens it again. The men are still
there, still smiling.*)

SECOND EVANGELIST: We're not trying to scare you.

FIRST EVANGELIST: No.

SECOND EVANGELIST: Do you understand the difference be-
tween righteousness and faith?

SHARON: Why don't you tell me.

SECOND EVANGELIST: It's only by the grace of God you'll be
saved.

SHARON: But what if I lead a good life? Does it still matter if I don't believe?

FIRST EVANGELIST: Do you really lead a good life?

SHARON: No.

SECOND EVANGELIST: You have to believe. If you don't, you go to Hell.

SHARON: Well, that doesn't seem fair.

FIRST EVANGELIST: I used to think that. But then I met Him.

SHARON: Who?

SECOND EVANGELIST: That's what we're trying to tell you.

FIRST EVANGELIST (*from John 3:16*): For God so loved the world that he gave his only begotten Son. That whosoever should believe in Him should not perish but have everlasting life.

SECOND EVANGELIST: You can have what we have.

FIRST EVANGELIST: A personal relationship with the Son of God.

SECOND EVANGELIST: It's hard to believe unless you believe it. But when you believe it, then it's easy. You just know.

SHARON: What?

FIRST EVANGELIST: Him.

SHARON: How?

FIRST EVANGELIST: Who knows? It just is.

SHARON: Right. And I'm supposed to buy this?

(*He hands her a small Bible.*)

FIRST EVANGELIST: No. It's a gift.

SECOND EVANGELIST: We know what you're thinking . . . It doesn't make sense.

SHARON: No.

SECOND EVANGELIST: I was like you.

SHARON: I doubt it.

SECOND EVANGELIST: No, really.

SHARON: And, like I said, I doubt it.

(*The men turn and leave. As they walk away,* SHARON *speaks:*)

SHARON: I heard someone talking about The Boy? Who's The Boy?

SECOND EVANGELIST: Some people say that he's a prophet in the old tradition.

FIRST EVANGELIST: And some people say there are others like him, all around the country.

SECOND EVANGELIST: All around the world.

SHARON: And what do you say?

SECOND EVANGELIST: I say trust in God.

(*The* SECOND EVANGELIST *gives* SHARON *a warm smile.*)

SHARON: Excuse me.

(*And she shuts the door.*

Cut to:)

INTERIOR: TELEPHONE COMPANY INFORMATION OFFICE. DAY.

SHARON *works at a computer terminal. Close on her.*

SHARON: Operator 134. What city please? (*Pause.*) City please? (*Pause.*) Please hold for the number. (*Pause.*) Operator 134. What city please? (*Pause.*) Is that a business or residence?

EXTERIOR/INTERIOR: SHARON'S APARTMENT. DAY.

The phone rings. She picks up, and we hear VIC *on the line.*

SHARON: Hello?

VIC (*voice-over*): Sharon?

SHARON: Hi, Vic.

VIC (*voice-over*): I dropped by a few of the hotels near the airport today. You'll never guess who I found. The most fascinating couple, really. They're from Philadelphia. Well, he's from Pennsylvania and she's from Florida and they're married. Isn't that romantic?

(*She sees evangelists pass outside on bicycles.*)

SHARON: What time?

VIC (*voice-over*): Pick you up at nine.

*   *   *

EXTERIOR: VIC'S WIFE'S HOUSE. NIGHT.
SHARON *looking out. Behind her,* VIC *is dancing with* ANGIE *and the* EXECUTIVE.

INTERIOR: VIC'S WIFE'S HOUSE. NIGHT.

EXECUTIVE: Here's to open-minded people and L.A., my kind of town.

ANGIE: Don't you have, uhh, (*to her husband while she corners* VIC) something better to do?

EXECUTIVE: I'm doing it.

(ANGIE *laughs as the* EXECUTIVE *goes to* SHARON. *She declines. Sharon's point of view as he walks back to the group.* VIC *dances with* ANGIE *while the* EXECUTIVE *gropes her a little. The* EXECUTIVE *unzips the back of Angie's dress as he turns her around, and as the dress falls away,* SHARON *can see a tattoo through the veil of Angie's long black hair.*

The tattoo is not finished: we see a long boat with an angel blowing a horn on the bow. Behind the scene is a large pearl.)

SHARON: What is that?

VIC: What are you talking about?

SHARON: She has a tattoo on her back.

(VIC *looks.*)

VIC: Whoa.

ANGIE: I got it when I was a kid.

EXECUTIVE: This was before she met me.

ANGIE: I got drunk one night.

SHARON: One night. You had it done in one night?

EXECUTIVE: Well, you know how kids are. I almost got a tattoo once. She was drunk.

(ANGIE *wraps herself around* VIC. *The naked* EXECUTIVE *fondles* SHARON *while she watches* VIC *and* ANGIE *kiss and laugh. The* EXECUTIVE *wants to get inside her, but she won't let him, he can only use his hands. For a moment, she enjoys it, but the pearl on Angie's back is too compelling.*)

SHARON: Angie, you got that in one night?

VIC: Maybe she doesn't want to talk about it.

ANGIE: There's nothing to talk about.

SHARON: Why did you get it?

VIC: Sharon? Can we talk about it later?

SHARON: I mean it must have been painful.

(ANGIE *realizes she has to deal with Sharon's curiosity.*)

ANGIE (*facing* SHARON): I don't remember, and I don't know why I got it.

(*She looks at the* EXECUTIVE. *He gives her a compassionate look.*)

EXECUTIVE: It's okay, Angie. I'm here. I'm with you.

SHARON: Why would you get a tattoo that you didn't really want? I'm sorry, I don't want to make you unhappy, but I really need to know.

ANGIE: Why?

SHARON: I don't know. I don't know. It's important. (*She asks again:*) What is it?

ANGIE: Don't you know what's going on?

SHARON: What?

ANGIE: The dream? The Pearl?

SHARON: What dream?

EXECUTIVE: Tell them.

(*Cut to:*)

INTERIOR: TELEPHONE COMPANY VENDING-MACHINE ROOM. DAY.

The three workers are sitting together, drinking coffee. SHARON *comes into the room and walks over to them, then sits down. She acts as though she's seen the light, but she's heavy-handed and obvious.*

SHARON: Hi, it's a beautiful day, isn't it? How are you?

WORKER #1 (*cautious*): We're fine. And you?

SHARON: I'm fine. Now that I dream about the Pearl.

(*Silence. The men watch her carefully. She becomes uncomfortable, but they don't release her from their hard stares. She is being evaluated.*)

WORKER #2: What dream would that be?

SHARON: The Pearl. I dream about the Pearl.

WORKER #3: Tell us about it.

WORKER #1: What does it look like?

SHARON: You know. The Pearl. It's a big pearl by a river.

WORKER #3: No, it's not.

WORKER #1: You haven't seen it.

SHARON: Yes, I have.

WORKER #2: You can't fake it.

(SHARON *slumps, defeated.*)

WORKER #1: It's a message from God. If you really want it, all you have to do is pray.

SHARON (*disdainfully*): Pray.

WORKER #2: He's coming back.

SHARON: Slow down. If everybody is getting this dream, how come it isn't on the news?

WORKER #2: Those who need to know, know.

WORKER #1: And those who don't believe won't get the dream.

SHARON: There are five billion people on the planet. There's I-don't-know-how-many religions. Why does the God of some little country on the Mediterranean have to be the God for everyone? Isn't that a little arrogant? I mean, really? The Buddhists get along okay without Jesus Christ. The Hindus get along okay without Jesus Christ. The Moslems seem to be getting along okay without Jesus Christ.

WORKER #1: But none of them are saved.

(*Cut to:*)

INTERIOR: SHARON'S APARTMENT. NIGHT.

SHARON *comes in. She goes to the bedroom.* VIC *is in bed with a woman.*

VIC: Sharon, this is my friend Andrea. Andrea is from Nebraska. Come and join?

(SHARON *leaves and slumps down a wall in the next room.*)

EXTERIOR: SHARON'S APARTMENT. DAY.

SHARON *smokes on the balcony. Something has changed.*

* * *

INTERIOR: SHARON'S APARTMENT. BEDROOM. NIGHT.
SHARON *wakes up. She shakes* RANDY.

> SHARON: Get up.
>
> RANDY: What?
>
> SHARON: Get up, or get out.
>
> RANDY: What did I do?
>
> SHARON: I have to make the bed.
>
> RANDY: Come on, look, no, it's three o'clock in the morning.
>
> SHARON: Get out of bed, or get out of the house.
>
> RANDY: Why?
>
> SHARON: This bed is unclean.
>
> RANDY: I'm out, I'm out. Unclean . . . you changed the sheets yesterday.
>
> SHARON: Shut up!

(And he gets out of bed. She rips the sheets off the bed and then we cut to:

Close-up of clean sheets being put over the bed. RANDY *isn't helping; he leans against a wall, trying to sleep.)*

> SHARON: I'm starting over, Randy. I've had enough.
>
> RANDY: Enough what?
>
> SHARON: I need a new direction in my life. There is a God, I know it, there is a God, and I'm going to meet Him.
>
> RANDY: When did you get religion?
>
> SHARON: I am trying, Randy. I want my salvation.
>
> RANDY: Sharon, you're fine the way you are.
>
> SHARON: You just want to live in sin, don't you?
>
> RANDY: That's right. I just want to live in sin.
>
> SHARON: Fine, be a slave to the Devil.
>
> RANDY: Devil? Do you remember where we met? Don't start asking me now to apologize for who I am or what I believe in.
>
> SHARON: Oh, and what do you believe in?
>
> RANDY: There is no God. There's only chaos.

* * *

INTERIOR: SHARON'S APARTMENT. BATHROOM. NIGHT.

SHARON *takes a shower.* RANDY *talks to her through the glass.*

SHARON: And why do we have such guilty consciences? Answer that?

RANDY: You're the one with the guilty conscience. I sleep really well, or at least I used to. (*He tests the shower water.*) Jesus Christ, that's hot.

SHARON: Don't take the Lord's name in vain, Randy. That's one of the commandments, it even comes before theft and adultery, it even comes before murder. That's how important it is not to take the Lord's name in vain.

RANDY: Since when have you known the Lord?

SHARON: I am trying to.

RANDY: And what does a shower at three in the morning have to do with eternal salvation?

(SHARON *is washing herself in a steaming hot shower. She scrubs herself with a hard brush. She gets out of the shower.*)

SHARON: I want to be clean. Am I clean?

(RANDY *watches in silence as she dries herself with a towel, cleans her fingernails, and brushes her teeth. She speaks to him in her reflection.*)

RANDY: Yeah, you're clean.

SHARON: When you do something wrong, we feel bad, and that's because there's a little bit of God in all of us, telling us to change our ways before it's too late. Isn't that right?

RANDY: No, it's not right. It's just conditioned by society. All we are is animals whose brains have become too big and too complicated for the purposes of satisfying our animal needs, which are food and sex.

SHARON: There is a spiritual need which is just as real as hunger, just as real as the need for love.

RANDY: Sharon, don't you understand what's going on? The world's a disaster. We have no power to make it better. You hate your job. You hate your life. But you want to feel special. But instead of letting me do that, you're rushing off to something that's not even there. There's no Pearl, there's only us.

(SHARON *flosses her teeth*.)

SHARON: I feel sorry for you, Randy, I really do. But you have to leave.

RANDY: I don't want to leave. I want to stay here with you. You know me. We know each other. We know each other's secrets, that's something. I think we can love each other, and I think you feel that too.

SHARON: There has to be something more.

RANDY: Why?

(SHARON *cries*.)

SHARON: I'm tired of the pain in my life. I'm tired of feeling empty all the time.

RANDY: Let me help you.

SHARON: Why can't we let God help both of us?

RANDY: Because there is no God.

(*And he is out the door. Hold on* SHARON.)

EXTERIOR: DRIVEWAY. NIGHT.

RANDY *gets into his truck.*

Cut to:

INTERIOR: SHARON'S APARTMENT. BEDROOM. NIGHT.

SHARON *reads the Bible the* EVANGELISTS *gave her and then simply clutches it.*

She tries to sleep, to relax.

Her eyes close.

Whatever it is, self-consciousness or doubt, she can't force herself to believe.

SHARON (*whispers*): God, please, please, please help me.
God, I'm lost.

(*Cut to:*)

* * *

EXTERIOR: ENDLESS BOULEVARD. DAY.

SHARON *drives aimlessly. She stops for a hitchhiker named* TOMMY, *rough-looking, with a bedroll and a rucksack.*
Cut to:

INTERIOR: SHARON'S CAR. DAY.

TOMMY: Chicks don't usually stop for me. (*No response from* SHARON.) In fact, I think they think I'm dangerous. (*Pause, again no response.*) They're probably right. I'm not as dangerous as some guys I know, but I would never give myself a lift, that's for sure. No way. If I was a chick, no double-fucking way would I give me a lift. I've looked in the mirror. I've seen myself. I mean, with my thumb out, if I was a chick and I saw me, no sir. On the other hand, if I was a, if I was the one who was hitching and I was a chick, I'd stop for me in a second. In fact, I'd, I'd fuck me, too. In fact, if I was hitching and I was a chick, and I got stopped by a chick, I'd fuck me that way, too. Yeah. In fact, I wouldn't mind getting into a bi-girl scene with myself. Actually, you're the first chick that has ever given me a lift. I think other chicks don't pick me up because they can tell I carry a gun and I've been to prison in Vermont. I don't think they can tell I've been to prison, but that's where I'm from. Vermont. You ever been to Vermont? (SHARON *doesn't answer.*) I'm from the Lemon Fair Valley. Actually, there's no lemons in Vermont. Actually, it comes from the French, *Lay Moan Vayer,* which means the Green Mountains. Which is what Vermont means. Green Mountains. *Vert:* Green. *Mont:* Mountains. Vermont. Green Mountains. Anyway, my father's a farmer. I left home. What's your name? I'm Tommy.
SHARON: Sharon.
TOMMY: Oh yeah? With who?
SHARON: What?
TOMMY: Who you sharin' it with? You gonna share it with me?
(*Cut to:*)

*   *   *

EXTERIOR: ADULT MOTEL. DAY.
Tracking shot past the entrance. Sharon's is not the only car parked at the motel.

INTERIOR: ADULT MOTEL. DAY.
TOMMY *is on the round bed. He plays with a knife. We hear the shower running. The camera peeks into the bathroom.*

INTERIOR: ADULT MOTEL. BATHROOM. DAY.
SHARON *is in the shower, dressed. Tommy's rucksack is just outside the bathroom.*
> TOMMY: Sharon? Did you know that the state bird of Vermont is the Hermit Thrush? I'll bet you didn't know that. The state flower is the Red Clover. Highest point is Mount Mansfield, I believe, which is four thousand three hundred ninety-three something, I don't know. Hey, have you got a quarter? Let's get some magic finger going in here. How would that be?

INTERIOR: ADULT MOTEL. DAY.
SHARON *pulls a gun from Tommy's rucksack. He hears something, turns.* SHARON *is standing there dripping, with the gun.*
> SHARON: It's time for you to go.
> TOMMY: Uhhh?
> SHARON: You have to go, Tommy, and you have to leave me your gun.
> TOMMY: Ahhhh!
(TOMMY *raises his knife, she cocks the gun, and he plunges it into the bed.*
Dissolve to:)

*   *   *

EXTERIOR/INTERIOR: ADULT MOTEL. LATER.

SHARON *is in bed, the blankets pulled up over her head. She pulls the blankets down. She reaches beside her for her bag. She opens her bag. A pint of pear schnapps.*

She drinks half the schnapps. She takes the gun and puts it under her chin. She closes her eyes and holds the gun for a long moment. She opens her eyes.

The disorder of the room bothers her.

She gets out of the bed and puts everything from the bag but the gun back into it. The ashtray on the night table is filled with crushed butts. She pulls the drawer open to hide the ashtray, and she finds the Gideon Bible. She puts the ashtray on top of the Bible.

She is a bit disgusted with herself, disappointed at her lack of resolve. Then she takes the Bible out of the drawer and opens it.

She starts to read the Gospels.

A golden light fills the room.

SHARON *is thrown backward by it, and before she's eclipsed by its brilliance:*

Dissolve to:

Extreme close-up: a pearl.

You've never seen a pearl this close, so close that we lose its shape. *All we can see of it is the color: the changing white, silver, and pink. It is beautiful. You don't want it to go away.*

Dissolve to:

INTERIOR: SHARON'S APARTMENT. DAY.

SHARON *is sleeping, smiling, at peace. She wakes up. Everything is different.*

She gets up. She goes to her closet and takes a simple dress from a hanger.

She hears a door. VIC *is behind her. She covers herself with the dress.*

> SHARON: Can I get dressed?
> VIC: Where were you?
> SHARON: Turn around.
> VIC: Really?

(She nods. He does while she puts on the dress.)

VIC: C'mon. Where have you been?

SHARON: I went away for a few days.

VIC: Who'd you go with?

SHARON: No one.

VIC: Meet anyone?

SHARON: Yes, yes, I did. I did meet someone.

(VIC *can sense that something is different about her by the way she talks to him so directly and so calmly, and by her placid smile.* VIC *lies on the bed. She comes out from behind the door.*)

VIC: Are you okay?

SHARON: I'm fine, Vic. I'm really, really fine.

VIC: Unnh-uhh. No you're not. Something's going on. You've changed. You've got this look right now.

SHARON: What look?

VIC: That goofy smile.

SHARON: If I tell you, you're not going to believe me. But I have to tell you, so it really doesn't matter if you don't believe me. It doesn't matter to me. I mean it matters to me, but you're the one who really needs to hear this now.

VIC: You met a guy.

SHARON: Well, *guy* is not exactly the word I'd use for Him.

VIC: You fox, you fell in love.

SHARON (*deadly serious*): Yes.

VIC: Wait until he finds out about you.

SHARON: Well, He knows all about me.

VIC: Is he as bad a boy as I am?

SHARON: I think you should meet Him.

VIC: Did you tell him about me?

SHARON: I told you, He knows everything.

VIC: He's rich, right? He's some rich guy, and you fell for some line of his.

SHARON: You could love Him, too.

VIC (*laughing*): Oh, no, you fell in love with some rich homosexual.

SHARON: He's the Lord Jesus Christ, Vic. He's the Son of God.

(VIC *jumps off the bed.*)

Vic: Sharon, did you quit your job?

Sharon: Why would I do that?

Vic: So you can go to the airport and sell flowers, or do whatever the cult wants you to do.

Sharon: You can't understand, but I know what that's like. Until it happens to you, until you accept God into your heart, it's like a fairy tale, it's like some joke that you just don't get.

Vic: I think you need to be deprogrammed.

Sharon: There's no cult, Vic. There's only God, and his message of Love.

Vic: Love.

Sharon: Love.

Vic: Look, you'll give this up, someday. I know you, you'll give this up.

Sharon: This is forever.

Vic: Everybody says that.

Sharon: This is different.

Vic: Everybody says that, too. (*He is heading out the door.*) Sharon, call me when this is over.

(Sharon *is alone, content.*

Cut to:)

INTERIOR: TELEPHONE COMPANY INFORMATION OFFICE. DAY.

Go down the rows of computer terminals, hearing other operators. Stop at Sharon.

Sharon: Hold for the number. Hi. Who's this? . . . Hi, Susanna, this is Sharon. Have you met Jesus? . . . Well, I'm sure you're in a hurry, but don't you think you could take time out to get to know your Lord and Savior? . . . well okay, well, you have a good day too. What was the number you wanted? Here you go . . . (*Pause.*) Hi, this is Sharon. Who's this? Hi, Maria. Have you met God? You have? Isn't He wonderful?

(*She looks up and sees* Henry, *her supervisor.*

Cut to:)

* * *

INTERIOR: TELEPHONE COMPANY. HENRY'S OFFICE. DAY.
The door is closed.

HENRY: You're supposed to spend a maximum of fifteen seconds on each call. Do you know what your average has been?

SHARON: No.

HENRY: Take a guess.

SHARON: Twenty seconds? Twenty-five?

HENRY: Two minutes. You were clocked on one call at seven minutes fifteen.

SHARON: I am just trying to do my job.

HENRY: It seems like you're trying to do two jobs.

SHARON (*a little defiantly*): We only have one job.

HENRY: That's right. And you're not doing the one you're being paid for.

SHARON: Henry, God made me an information operator for a reason. I'm in a position to spread His word to hundreds of people every day, personally. One-to-one.

HENRY: God.

SHARON: I know you can't believe this, but God is coming back to judge the world. And it's important, I have to tell people. We have to prepare for His return.

(HENRY *takes his time before speaking.*)

HENRY: When did you first see the light?

SHARON: A few days ago.

HENRY (*neutral*): Mmm-hmm.

SHARON: You don't believe me.

HENRY: Sometimes people have heard about the Pearl and they try to pretend like they've seen it, but you can always tell when they're lying. You just can't fake it.

SHARON: You?

(SHARON *puts her hand on her heart.*)

HENRY: When they first meet Him, everyone thinks that Judgement Day is just around the corner. I remember that feeling very well; it's a powerful feeling. But . . . that sense that it's going to happen tomorrow passes when tomorrow comes and He doesn't. And then you understand that those feelings, as powerful as they are, and the dreams, as real as they are, are still just shadows of the real thing, and no one can say how far away that real thing really is.

SHARON: The feeling is so strong.

(HENRY *studies her.*)

HENRY: I don't know you, but I know you. A lot of people who have come to God are broken. They've been messed up by life. The unbelievers try to make it seem like there's something wrong with us, that we're stupid, but only the humble hear the voice of God. You're alone, aren't you?

SHARON (*tears forming*): Yes.

HENRY: It's hard at the beginning. You give up your old life, and it's like you've come to a new country. Your old friends can not really be your friends anymore.

SHARON: What do I do?

HENRY: Trust in God, and take it easy on the phones.

(SHARON *smiles.*)

SHARON: Who's The Boy?

(*He looks at her.*

Cut to:)

INTERIOR: CHURCH. DAY.

A small, spare room. No pews, only a circle of folding chairs. Perhaps twenty people are there. We're watching HENRY *and his son,* THE BOY, *about ten years old. He never speaks out loud; he whispers behind a cupped hand into his father's ear.*

On SHARON, *across from them, watching.*

On THE BOY: *he cups a hand and speaks to* HENRY. HENRY *addresses the room.*

HENRY: God is coming back. There are wars and rumors of wars, and a curse devours the Earth, and those who live in it are held guilty.

Robert Altman (Lorey Sabastian, © 1992 Fine Line Features)

Detective Avery (Whoopi Goldberg) and Griffin Mill (Tim Robbins) (Lorey Sabastian, © 1992 New Line Cinema Corp.)

Griffin Mill (Tim Robbins) and June Gudmundsdottir (Greta Scacchi) (Lorey Sabastian, © 1992 New Line Cinema Corp.)

Sharon (Mimi Rogers) (Abigayle Tarsches, © 1991 New Line Cinema Corp.)

Vic (Patrick Bauchau) and Sharon (Mimi Rogers) (Abigayle Tarsches, © 1991 New Line Cinema Corp.)

Sharon (Mimi Rogers) and Mary (Kimberly Cullum) (Abigayle Tarsches, © 1991 New Line Cinema Corp.)

"Those who need to know, know."
From left to right: The Older Boy (Christian Belnavis), Henry (Dick Anthony Williams), and Vic (Patrick Bauchau) (Abigayle Tarsches, © 1991 New Line Cinema Corp.)

"With enough condoms."
Peter Witner (Peter Weller), Bettina (Tanya Pohlkotte). In the background
is the Other Katherine (Kimberly Kates). (K. C. Bailey, © 1994 Warner Bros.
Prod. Ltd. and Monarchy Enterprises, C.V.)

Katherine Witner (Judy Davis) (K. C. Bailey, © 1994 Monarchy Enterprises, C.V.)

From left to right: Alison Gale (Paula Marshall), Katherine Witner (Judy Davis), and Peter Witner (Peter Weller) (K. C. Bailey, © 1994 Monarchy Enterprises, C.V.)

From left to right: Peter Weller, John Campbell (director of photography), and Michael Tolkin (K. C. Bailey, © 1994 Warner Bros. Prod. Ltd. and Monarchy Enterprises, C.V.)

"Have you ever seen a man? This is a man."
Dale Deveaux (Samuel L. Jackson) and Peter Witner (Peter Weller) (K. C. Bailey,
© 1994 Monarchy Enterprises, C.V.)

Peter leaves the party early.
From left to right: Peter Witner (Peter Weller), Bob (Bob Flanagan on the bed of
nails), Victoria (Victoria Baker), and Bob's Friend (Sheree Rose) (K. C. Bailey, © 1994
Monarchy Enterprises, C.V.)

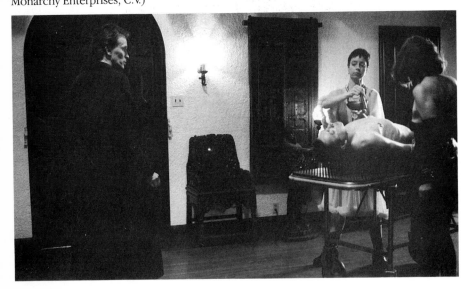

(THE BOY *again whispers to his father.*)

    HENRY: We have to wait.

(An OLDER WOMAN *in the circle.*)

    SHARON: For how long?

(THE BOY *whispers to his father.*)

    HENRY: Probably a few years. Five years, six years.

(*The people in the room hug each other.* SHARON *gives herself to the hugs and gives hugs. Love without sex.*

Dissolve to:)

INTERIOR: RANDY'S WORKPLACE.

RANDY *sprays coating on a metal gate.* SHARON *arrives.*

    SHARON: Hi, Randy.

    RANDY (*pretends to struggle to remember her name*): Ohh, uhh, Sharon. Sharon. How's that apartment coming? Is it still unclean?

    SHARON: No.

    RANDY: So you found your salvation. Congratulations.

    SHARON: I found God.

    RANDY: Oh yeah? Is he going to move in, or did he keep his own place, or are you going to do that commuting thing? You've got to watch that; it's very tough on a relationship. Why are you here?

(*They walk into an adjoining woodshop.*)

    SHARON: I know you are as lost as I was, Randy, and I wanted to tell you that you could know God. If you just surrender your pride, you can know God.

    RANDY: Sharon, it's just a drug. Instead of doing heroin, you're doing God, and I need sandpaper.

    SHARON: Randy, God is real. God is not make-believe, and you know that. You don't want to admit that, because you're afraid.

    RANDY: What am I afraid of?

    SHARON: What we are all afraid of: God's judgement.

    RANDY: No. I'm not.

    SHARON: I don't want to lose you.

RANDY: You just want to save my soul.

SHARON: At least you know you have one.

RANDY: I don't want to tell my secrets in church.

SHARON: I'll pray for both of us.

RANDY: You'd stay with me even if I didn't pray?

(SHARON *kisses* RANDY. *They hug.*)

TITLE SUPERIMPOSED: SIX YEARS LATER

INTERIOR: CHURCH. NIGHT.

There are more people in the room now. THE BOY *is older now; and although* HENRY *is beside him, he speaks directly.*

THE BOY: So far, we're still in the realm of signs and wonders . . . But the Rapture is coming. It says so in the Bible. Our bodies will be transformed into spirit. And then we will be caught up in a cloud to meet God. The end is coming soon . . . This year . . .

(RANDY *takes Sharon's hand.*

Cut to:)

INTERIOR: SHARON AND RANDY'S TOWN HOUSE. BEDROOM. NIGHT.

The bedroom is now filled with Christian icons. SHARON *and* RANDY *wake up together, shaken by the same image.*

RANDY: Ever since I was a kid, I've had the feeling that something was going to happen to me. I always knew that when it happened, I would recognize it, and that I wouldn't mistake it for something else. I wouldn't have something happen to me and I would say, this is it! and then later on say, no, that wasn't it. It was a secret feeling, and I never told anybody about it.

SHARON: And what's the feeling now?

RANDY: Something's going to happen.

*   *   *

INTERIOR: RANDY AND SHARON'S KITCHEN. DAY.

SHARON *and her daughter,* MARY, *six years old, sit at the kitchen table.*

>   MARY: Where's Heaven?
>   SHARON: It's in the sky.
>   MARY: Why can't we see it?
>   SHARON: You will.
>   MARY: But why can't we see it now?
>   SHARON: Mary? Do you love Baby Jesus?
>   MARY: Yes.
>   SHARON: Then you'll see him really soon.

(*Slowly dissolve to:*)

EXTERIOR: SWIMMING POOL. DAY.

We move through the water, and the change from the light is easy, gradual. The water is ethereal; we don't even know this is a pool yet; it could be a body of heavenly water. The calm surface of the pool explodes as a six-year-old-girl, MARY, *bursts to the surface.* SHARON *moves through the water. Her friend* PAULA *floats on a raft.*

>   PAULA: What does the Bible say?
>   SHARON: We who are alive who are saved will be taken bodily into Heaven.
>   PAULA: Ohhh, Sharon . . . Sharon . . .
>   SHARON: You can't accept God, can you?
>   PAULA: No.
>   SHARON: Well, maybe we should talk about that for a minute.
>   PAULA (*smiling*): Okay, do you mean that if you're a Christian and you're ironing your shirts and the Rapture happens, you'll be taken to Heaven in the middle of doing the laundry? Or does God give you time to turn off the iron, or do your shirts burn?
>   SHARON (*joking but deadpan*): I wear permanent press.
>   PAULA: Well, I mean what's supposed to happen? You are supposed to float up into the sky?
>   SHARON: In the twinkling of an eye. The body will be

transformed into spirit. And there is a warning. If you
listen, if you pray for it. We'll hear the sound of trumpets,
God's angels.

(MARY *listens.*)

INTERIOR: RANDY'S WORKPLACE. DAY.

RANDY *is now a supervisor in a large insurance office. He is well
groomed; his hair is cut short; he is a few pounds lighter. Other work-
ers are around.* RANDY *is arguing with* LOUIS, *another worker. A secu-
rity officer stands behind* RANDY.

RANDY: Louis, I'm trying to say this without causing you a
lot of pain.

LOUIS: Any way you say it, I'm fired, right?

RANDY: We have struggled together, but, you have to
admit, it hasn't worked out.

LOUIS: That's because I'm not kissing ass around here,
isn't it?

RANDY: Louis, it's because you're not doing your job.

LOUIS: You're not doing your job, banana-head.

RANDY: Louis, we've tried to help you, haven't we?

LOUIS (*crying*): I don't want your fucking help.

RANDY: We took you to a counselor.

LOUIS: You took me to a homo.

RANDY: I took you to an A.A. meeting.

LOUIS: They were a bunch of a-holes. A-holes Anony-
mous. And you're an a-hole. And I'm tired of kissing your
Christian a-hole. (*To the security guard:*) What are you
looking at?

RANDY: Louis, I'll pray for you.

LOUIS (*wildly*): Yeah, well, fuck you!

(*Cut to:*)

INTERIOR: RANDY AND SHARON'S APARTMENT. DAY.

MARY *and her parents,* RANDY *and* SHARON, *hold hands in a circle.
This is a happy family.*

* * *

INTERIOR: RANDY'S WORKPLACE. DAY.

We hear a blast. We see RANDY *in his office at the corner of a hall. There are two bodies in the hall, and* LOUIS *walks down it with a gun.* RANDY *gets up from his desk and starts to come out. As he does,* LOUIS *shoots into an office.* LOUIS *goes into another office, and we hear two more shotgun blasts.* RANDY *is now out of his office and turning down the empty hall when* LOUIS *comes back into the hall.*

RANDY: Louis.

LOUIS: No speeches, preacher.

RANDY: I have a little girl.

LOUIS: So what?

(*And he blasts* RANDY.)

Cut to:)

INTERIOR: SHARON AND RANDY'S TOWN HOUSE. DAY.

MARY *opens the front door.*

MARY: Come in.

(*The living room is filled with friends who have brought food to* SHARON. MARY *and other children play.* SHARON *talks to* PAULA *on a balcony.*)

PAULA: You see, now's one of those times when I wish I was a believer.

SHARON: Why?

PAULA: Because I would have a rock to stand on, because I could tell myself that everything was for the better because God has a plan.

SHARON: But it is, because He does.

PAULA: It is so hard for me, Sharon. I try to resist it as much as possible.

SHARON: So you do feel something tugging at you, don't you?

PAULA: I tell myself it's just conditioning, it's how I was raised. I tell myself that if we didn't tell our children about

God, they wouldn't ask. It is a story we tell ourselves so
everything makes sense.
SHARON: It's not.
PAULA: But how do you know?
SHARON: The Bible.
PAULA: Don't tell me the Bible.
SHARON: It's a question of faith.
PAULA: So there's no proof?
SHARON: Paula, the universe you live in is cold and filled
with empty space. The universe I live in is filled with God.

(*Cut to:*)

INTERIOR: SHARON AND RANDY'S TOWN HOUSE. NIGHT.
SHARON *and* MARY *kneel at Mary's bed, praying.*
MARY: Will we see Daddy again?
SHARON: Yes.
MARY: When we die?
SHARON: Or when God takes us to Heaven.
MARY: When the Rapture comes, does that mean we die?
SHARON: Not exactly.
MARY: So you can go to Heaven without dying?
SHARON: Yeah.
MARY: But if you die, you can still go to Heaven.
SHARON: Yes.
MARY: So Daddy is going to Heaven.
SHARON: No, Daddy's already in Heaven.
MARY: If we pray to Daddy, can he hear us?
SHARON: Well, we pray to God, and God tells Daddy what
we're saying. That way he can hear everything.

(*Cut to:*)

EXTERIOR: MINIMALL STAIRCASE. DAY.
SHARON *comes down the stairs and stops.*
Pull back to reveal:
We are outside a Photolab in a corner pod mall. SHARON *walks into
view, looking at the snapshots of America rolling off the printer.*

In the photographs, we see RANDY *wearing the clothes in which he died, and he's trying to reach her, trying to say something to her. Her husband appears improbably in a picture at the beach, standing behind a typical family. Then* RANDY *is pictured in the desert, standing on a tall rock pile, his arm raised, calling her to him. He's pleading with her.*
Cut to:

INTERIOR: CHURCH. DAY.
The room is filled; people are standing on chairs at the wall. There's still a circle in the middle, but it's smaller. HENRY *and* THE BOY *are flanked by the two* EVANGELISTS. SHARON *is across from them, with* MARY. *Now* THE BOY *speaks.*

THE BOY: This is from the Book of Revelation, chapter 12, verse 6. It says, "And the woman fled into the desert where she had a place prepared for her by God." Is anyone else getting visions that tell us we have to go to the desert?

SHARON: You don't believe me.

THE BOY: I do.

SHARON: What does it mean?

THE BOY: You're the only one who can hear these calls. It could be Satan.

SHARON: I don't think so.

THE BOY: Then God wants you for His special purpose.

SHARON: Please, come with me.

THE BOY: We haven't been invited.

(SHARON *wants to cry. She gets up and takes Mary's hand. The crowd parts for her, making a path to the door. She starts walking toward it, about ten feet.*)

SHARON: But I'm scared.

THE BOY: Don't ask God to meet you halfway.

SHARON: What does that mean?

(THE BOY *shakes his head no.*)

HENRY (*to* THE BOY): What does that mean?

(THE BOY *shakes his head. No, he won't answer.* SHARON *is scared. She opens the door.*)

* * *

EXTERIOR: OUTSIDE THE CHURCH. SUNSET.
SHARON *and* MARY *are framed in the church door, the faithful behind them. They walk out into the sunset.*
Cut to:

EXTERIOR: SHARON AND RANDY'S TOWN HOUSE. DAY.
SHARON *is packing a sports bag while* PAULA *watches her.* PAULA *is desperate.* SHARON *is calm.* SHARON *holds up a few of Mary's dresses while she studies the clothes in her closet.* PAULA *has a shopping bag filled with food.*

PAULA: Sharon, you can't just leave like this.

SHARON: Yes, I can. God is calling me.

PAULA: No, no, no . . . Sharon . . . what about Mary?

SHARON: God is calling her too.

PAULA: Why don't you sell the house? You can't just walk away from it.

SHARON: Of course, I can. There's a better house waiting for me. God is building me a mansion, right now. What should I wear?

(*She takes out a few dresses.*)

PAULA: God won't come, the bank will own your home, and what are you going to do then?

SHARON: I'm going to Heaven, Paula. I'm going to Heaven. Mary and I are going to Heaven. And we'll wear these dresses, together, when we finally meet God. Randy always liked this dress. I'll wear it for him. I'll be seeing him soon. And he always loved to see Mary in this.

(PAULA *sits on the bed.*)

PAULA: Don't you get a white robe and wings?

SHARON: Angels don't have wings. And I don't know about the robes. I don't know what they wear, but I guess I'll find out.

(SHARON *packs a sweater.*)

PAULA: Then what's the sweater for?

SHARON: It gets cold at night in the desert.

PAULA: Winter is coming. You'll need more than a sweater.

SHARON: He's taking us soon, very soon.

PAULA: How do you know?

SHARON: He told me.

PAULA: Sharon, Sharon, listen to me. I don't know if you can hear me, but listen to me. You need food.

SHARON: Not that much.

PAULA: You need a tent. I don't want you guys sleeping out in the car. Okay. Candle, matches, flashlight.

(PAULA *pulls the named items out of the bag.*)

SHARON: Thank you, Paula.

PAULA: You need something else. You can't go out to the desert alone, there's a lot of creeps out there, Sharon, and a woman alone, I'm scared.

SHARON: God will take care of us.

PAULA: Maybe. Insurance.

(*She takes out a small handgun.*)

SHARON: Oh, Paula, no.

PAULA: You don't have to use it. But you have to take it. And you can bring it back to me when you come home.

(SHARON *holds Paula's hand, and she looks at the gun.*)

SHARON: I'm not coming home.

(*Cut to:*)

EXTERIOR: DESERT CAMPGROUND. DAY.

SHARON *and* MARY *drive into a campground somewhere in the high desert. There are Joshua trees, yuccas, and large rocks and rock piles.*

MARY: Mom?

SHARON: Yes, Mary.

MARY: This doesn't look like Heaven, Mom.

SHARON: This isn't Heaven, honey.

MARY: Then why stop here?

SHARON: Think of Heaven as a great big hotel or a big office building.

MARY: Yeah.

SHARON: Well, this is the lobby, this is where we have to wait.

MARY: For what?

SHARON: The elevator.

(*Another car pulls up.*

Dissolve to:)

INTERIOR: TENT. NIGHT.

SHARON *and* MARY *sleeping. We go into Sharon's dream. She is dreaming of the Pearl.*

Cut to:

EXTERIOR: DESERT CAMPGROUND. DAY.

ROCK CLIMBERS *are high on the sheer face of a rock wall.* MARY *watches them. One* CLIMBER *rappels down the rock and lands beside them. He is lean, muscular, cool.*

MARY: Are you waiting for God, too?

CLIMBER: Oh, is that what you guys are doing here?

MARY: God is coming back.

CLIMBER: Sounds good.

MARY: He really is.

CLIMBER: Okay.

MARY: He's coming tomorrow.

SHARON: No, soon, Mary. He's coming soon.

(*They look up at the sky.*)

EXTERIOR: DESERT CAMPGROUND. NIGHT.

SHARON *puts* MARY *to sleep in the tent.*

EXTERIOR: DESERT CAMPGROUND. LATE DAY.

There isn't much food left or water. We hear a loud siren. SHARON *grabs* MARY. MARY *grabs for her toy panda.*

SHARON: That's it! That's it, Mary, here it comes, here it is,
he's calling us, come on, hurry, hurry . . .
(*She runs with* MARY *up a rock formation, higher and higher. The*
sound continues. MARY *drops her panda and screams out:*)
MARY: Panda!
SHARON: Mary, come on . . .
MARY: No, Panda!
(SHARON *scrambles back to get the doll. It is out of reach. She gets it.*
MARY *hugs her panda, and they continue on up the rock until we*
have a good view of the whole campground.)

EXTERIOR: TOP OF ROCK PILE. DAY.
The horn is still loud and clear. SHARON *holds* MARY, *their faces lifted*
to the sky, waiting for the Rapture. We see a CLIMBER *running across*
the parking lot to his car. He turns off the alarm, and the sound
stops. SHARON *remains frozen for a second; then she sits down. For*
the first time, we see real doubt and the beginning of defeat. MARY
starts to cry.
MARY: I miss my Daddy.
SHARON: Honey, I miss your Daddy, too.
MARY: I want to see him again.
SHARON: You will, you will see him in Heaven.
MARY: Why can't we go to Heaven? Mommy, I want to go
to Heaven.
SHARON: We have to wait until God calls us.
MARY: Did God call Daddy? When you die is that when
God calls you?
SHARON: Yes.
MARY: Then I want to die.
SHARON: No, sweetie, no.
MARY: You want to go to Heaven, don't you?
SHARON: Yes.
MARY: And you believe that when we die we'll go to
Heaven, because we're saved, right?
SHARON: Yes.
MARY: Then why can't we just die and go there really

quickly and be with Daddy again? Why do we have to
stay here and just hang around and wait for God? Come
on, Mom, let's die.

(SHARON *puts her arm around her. She is too young to really under-
stand what she's asking for.*)

SHARON: Let's give God one more chance.

(*Cut to:*)

EXTERIOR: DESERT CAMPGROUND. DAY.

A county sheriff's car drives into the campground. FOSTER MADISON
gets out of it. MARY *and* SHARON *pray at a picnic bench. Something
about* SHARON *attracts him. He could be hard, but he is curious, soft.*

FOSTER: Howdy.

SHARON: Hello.

FOSTER: I'm Foster Madison.

SHARON: Sharon. And Mary.

(FOSTER *crouches to be closer to* MARY.)

FOSTER: Oh yeah? I have a sister named Mary. She's all
grown-up now.

MARY: Are you with God?

FOSTER: I'm with the sheriff.

MARY: We're waiting for our father.

FOSTER: Where is he?

MARY: Heaven.

FOSTER: Don't you go to school?

MARY: I don't have to go to school.

(FOSTER *looks at* SHARON.)

SHARON: I'm not asking you to understand, or to have
faith, but the end of the world is coming, and we're a lot
safer out here.

(MARY *walks away.*)

FOSTER: Well, there's a two-week limit on staying here.

SHARON: Is that a limit on how long I can stay in the park,
or how long I can use this campsite?

FOSTER: Actually, it's just a limit on how long you can use
this particular campsite.

SHARON (*points to different campsites*): So if I move over there, or over there, or over there . . . I can stay for another two weeks.

(FOSTER *wants to be fair; he sees a woman in need.*)

FOSTER: Technically. I can't stop you.

SHARON: Thank you.

FOSTER: Could I ask you a question?

SHARON: Sure.

FOSTER: Is this good for your little girl?

SHARON: Have you been saved?

FOSTER: No.

SHARON: Do you know what that means?

FOSTER: Yeah.

SHARON: Would you like to be?

FOSTER: Oh yeah, yeah sure, who wouldn't.

SHARON: Why is it so hard for you to pray?

FOSTER: You have to surrender to God, don't you?

SHARON (*not fully certain*): That's right.

FOSTER: It's in my training. I don't give up my gun.

SHARON: But you'd like to believe.

FOSTER: That these are the last days?

SHARON: You know they are. God is coming back to judge the world. A lot of people are going to suffer.

FOSTER: I hope that's not true; but if there's no law against it, my hands are tied.

(SHARON *smiles a little.*)

SHARON: I bet with a little prayer you'd be on my side in an hour.

FOSTER: Well, then it's time for me to go. Watch out for the coyotes. (*To* MARY:) Good-bye.

MARY: Good-bye.

(FOSTER *gets back into his car. When he is gone,* SHARON *breaks down and cries.*)

EXTERIOR: DESERT CAMPGROUND. NIGHT.
The moon is behind clouds. Wind pulls at the tent flaps.

* * *

INTERIOR: TENT. NIGHT.

The camera moves toward SHARON. *We're getting inside her dream again. Brief glimpses of an orgy.*

INTERIOR: SHARON'S DREAM.

The Pearl recedes, gets smaller, and finally disappears.
Blackness.

> MARY (*voice-over*): Mom . . . Mommy . . .

INTERIOR: TENT. NIGHT.

SHARON *wakes up; her eyes are hollow.* MARY *is awake.*

> MARY: Mom . . .
> SHARON (*lost*): What?
> MARY: Mom, I'm hungry.

EXTERIOR: DESERT CAMPGROUND. DAY.

SHARON *looks through trash cans. No food. She turns the water jugs upside down. No water.* MARY *watches her.*

> MARY: You said we'd give him one more chance.
> SHARON (*impatient*): Who?
> MARY: God. You said you'd give God one more chance, and if we didn't get the Rapture that we could die. That's what you said. You promised.
> SHARON (*gently avoiding the question*): Baby . . .
> MARY: Don't you believe in God?
> SHARON: Yes.
> MARY: Don't you love God? Then why can't we just go to God? Go now. Now.

(SHARON *doesn't answer immediately.*)

> SHARON (*the implications are frightening*): One more chance.

(*Cut to:*)

* * *

EXTERIOR: DESERT CAMPGROUND. NIGHT.

A motorcycle comes into the campground. SHARON *and* MARY *are in the tent.* SHARON *pokes her head out. The motorcycle comes closer.* SHARON *gets out.*

FOSTER, *out of uniform, is on the motorcycle.*

> FOSTER: I . . . I was in the neighborhood.
>
> SHARON: And you thought you'd come by for a cup of sugar.
>
> FOSTER: No. Actually, I came to bring you this.

(He reaches into his pack for a blanket. He hands it to her.)

> SHARON: We have sleeping bags.
>
> FOSTER: Yeah, I know, I, it's just that sometimes you want to sit on the ground, you don't want to get dirty, it's nice to have a blanket.
>
> SHARON: Thank you.
>
> FOSTER: I, I brought your little girl a candy bar. I know moms are worried about cavities, so if you don't want to give it to her, you know, I'll understand.
>
> SHARON: I'll give it to her.
>
> FOSTER: You can share it.
>
> SHARON: Thanks.

(He wants to talk. He looks at her.)

> FOSTER: Well, I'll check up on you again sometime, if that's okay.
>
> SHARON: Thank you.

(And he rides away. She returns to the tent.)

INTERIOR: TENT. NIGHT.

Close on MARY. *She cries out in her sleep.*

> MARY: Mom! You have to make up your mind, now! Gabriel is coming, Mom, Gabriel is coming. *(She wakes up, and she is in a kind of trance, staring at her mother, afraid for her.)* He's God, Mom, He's God. Don't ask God to meet you halfway. *(A final cry.)* Mommy!

SHARON: Wake up, Mary, wake up. It's okay, baby, it's okay.

(MARY *wakes up, and she cries deeply. Her face tells us everything: she has given up hope.*)

SHARON: Come on, baby, you're just hungry; we'll get something to eat. Come on, let's go to town.

MARY: No, we can't leave.

SHARON: Yes, we can.

MARY: But we don't need any food. God will give us food when we get to Heaven. I'll be in Heaven tonight. There was a river. And I was in Heaven.

SHARON: Where was I?

MARY: You were there.

SHARON: Good.

MARY: Sort of. You were there, but only sort of.

(SHARON *tries to make sense of this. She can't; she's too tired right now for tests of faith. She smiles and looks her daughter in the eye.*)

SHARON: It's almost morning. As soon as the sun comes up, we'll go get something to eat.

(*Cut to:*)

EXTERIOR: JACK IN THE BOX DRIVE-THRU LINE. DAY.

SHARON *is at the pick-up window. The food order is put out for her. The* CASHIER *waits for the money. Behind him is the* MANAGER.

CASHIER: Eleven dollars and twenty-eight cents, please.

(SHARON *looks at him. He knows what the look means.*)

CASHIER: Oh, no you don't.

(SHARON *quickly grabs the food and drives away.*)

CASHIER: Call the police.

MANAGER: No.

CASHIER: Why not?

MANAGER: She had a kid.

INTERIOR: CAR. DAY.

SHARON *returns to the Joshua tree campsite.* MARY *devours her burger and fries. Sharon's face is set. She is on the other side of something powerful.*

EXTERIOR: CAR. DAY.
SHARON *drives down a road.*

EXTERIOR: BURNED HILL. LATE AFTERNOON.
SHARON *and* MARY *walk up the hillside.* MARY *kneels and clutches her toy panda.* SHARON *stands behind her.*

SHARON: Do you love me?

MARY: Yes.

SHARON: Do you love Jesus?

MARY: Yes.

SHARON: You know, in Heaven there's Jesus and Baby Jesus, together, and Baby Jesus has the special job, has the special job (*breaking down*) of looking out for all the children. Mary, do you love Baby Jesus?

MARY: Yes.

SHARON: It's not fair to make you pay because I'm lost. If God loves us, He'll understand. We're going to Heaven *now.*

MARY: We're going together?

SHARON: Together.

(*Now we see the gun that* PAULA *gave her before she left home. The sun is going down.*)

MARY: And Daddy? Daddy's in Heaven.

SHARON (*this thought comforts her*): Daddy. We'll see Daddy. Yes. And we'll be together forever because nothing is broken in Heaven. I love you.

MARY: Daddy.

SHARON: You have to love God, Mary, do you love God?

MARY: Yes.

(MARY *makes a face as though she's about to enter icy water. With her panda tucked under her arm, she clasps her hands in prayer even harder.*)

SHARON: Tell Him that. Don't be afraid.
(SHARON *pulls the trigger, and the gun fires.* MARY *is dead.*
SHARON *takes the gun and puts it to her head.*
She holds the gun. We watch. We wait. Will she? Can she? She emp-
ties the gun into the air, screams at the sky; then she sits down on the
ground; then she lies down beside MARY *and goes to sleep.*
Fade-out:
Fade-in:)

EXTERIOR: BURNED HILL. LATER. NIGHT.
SHARON *places a cross on the panda on top of the grave and then gets*
up. She walks away, empty.
We hear hoofbeats, one horse, distant. The sound gets louder.

INTERIOR: SHARON'S CAR. NIGHT.
SHARON *speeds down the highway, and everywhere she looks she sees*
a white horse flashing in her vision.
Cut to:

EXTERIOR: FREEWAY. NIGHT.
SHARON *keeps speeding. The white horse is gone. And then the red*
lights of a sheriff's police car appear in the mirror. The siren is close.
She is sure she has been caught. She pulls over. The sheriff is OFFICER
MADISON *from the campground. He shines his searchlight on*
Sharon's car. Then he walks to the car and knocks on her window.
    FOSTER: Could you get out of the car, please?
(SHARON *gets out of the car.*)
    FOSTER: What happened to God? (*He can see she is in*
        some kind of distress.) What's wrong?
(*She doesn't answer.*)
    FOSTER: I have to see your license and registration, please.
    SHARON: They're in the car.
(*She gets them. She holds the license and registration out in her*
hand.)

FOSTER: Thank you. Could you step over into the light, please?

(*He takes the identification and goes back to his bike.* SHARON *nods yes. He studies the license. We look at him for a moment. He is not a bad man, and he is studying* SHARON, *less as another speeder than as a woman in obvious trouble.*

In the beginning, SHARON *is catatonic; her answers are short and sparse. As* FOSTER *continues to press her, she starts to unravel. She realizes what she has done.*)

FOSTER: Here. Where's your little girl?

SHARON: She's with God.

FOSTER: She died?

SHARON: Yes.

FOSTER: Mary.

SHARON: Yes.

FOSTER: How?

SHARON: I killed her. I was going to kill myself too, but you can't get into Heaven if you kill yourself. You can get into Heaven if somebody else kills you but not if you kill yourself. Life is some kind of punishment, isn't it? You have to go through with it, even when you know what life is for.

FOSTER: What is life for?

SHARON: Ask God.

FOSTER: What does he say?

SHARON: I think He says that, basically, you have to love Him, no matter what. But I don't love Him, not anymore. He has too many rules. He told me to meet Him in the desert. And I did and I waited. He didn't come. He broke His promise. He let me kill my little girl. And He still expects me to love Him? I'm afraid of Hell, so I have to wait out my life, waiting for God. Now: He'll forgive me and He'll let me join my daughter and my husband in Heaven, but first I have to say I love Him. You can send me to the gas chamber, and if I let God into my heart before I die, then I can go to Heaven, because God is merciful. How fast was I going?

FOSTER: A hundred miles an hour.

SHARON: A hundred miles an hour. If I had gone off a bridge and died, would I have gone to Heaven?

FOSTER: I don't know.

SHARON: Neither do I.

(*Dissolve to:*)

INTERIOR: PRISON. DAY.

A guard leads SHARON *down a row of cells. A door is opened and then locked behind her. A woman on the next bed is reading the Bible, and when she lowers the book, we see it is* ANGIE, *the swinger with the tattoo.* SHARON *says nothing to her.*

ANGIE: I know you. I should be embarrassed to even tell you where we met, but I'm not ashamed, I'm not ashamed of anything anymore, I found God, God found me. I was preaching the word of God at a shopping mall in Palm Springs, and they had me kicked out. So I went back in, and they had me arrested. Have you heard the word of God? (*No reply.*) It's the greatest gift of all time. You have to trust completely in God. He'll forgive all your sins.

SHARON: Who forgives God?

(*And she turns away from her.*
Fade-out:)

INTERIOR: PRISON CELL. NIGHT.

SHARON *hears a sound from her cell. A flaming sword slices the air. The sword stops flaming when it cuts through the air. The sword is held by the* ARCHANGEL MICHAEL. ANGIE *sleeps.*

Another angel drifts into this scene outside the cell. MARY *appears dressed as she was when she died.*

MARY (*sincerely, with a little difficulty*): God is coming back, Mommy. There are wars and rumors of wars, Mommy, and a curse devours the Earth, and those who live in it are held guilty.

SHARON: He said He was going to take us to Heaven.

MARY: Mother, listen to me. The living outnumber the dead. The Armies of the Lord are waiting for the Day of Judgement. Don't you still love God, Mommy?

SHARON: He left us, alone, in the desert. He let me kill you.

MARY: Do you still love Him?

SHARON: How can I love a God who let me kill my baby?

MARY: God loves you because you love Him.

SHARON: Why?

MARY: I know you want me back, but I can't come back, Mommy. I'm dead.

(SHARON *looks as they vanish, then, after a beat, looks down. Cut to:*)

INTERIOR: PRISON. NIGHT.

We move through the cells. A trumpet plays one long, extended note. The prisoners look outside.

ANGIE: That's the first call. It's Gabriel blowing his trumpet. There will be six more calls. We have until the last call to repent. After that, it's too late. After that, it's too late.

(*We hear the hoofbeats again, getting louder. People look up. The sound seems to be in the middle of the room. The sound of the hoofbeats is impossibly loud, and we see on the TV screen the faint image of a white horse over a ball game. Then the game disappears, and we see the feet of the horse.*)

ANGIE: It's God. He's giving us a last chance to save ourselves. At war, the First Horseman of the Apocalypse.

(*The horse is replaced by a trumpet. The channels are changed, and the golden trumpet blowing the pure tone is seen across every channel. It is a long trumpet raised high before a deep blue background. A hand holds the trumpet, but we don't see the angel's face.* ANGIE *begins to sing:*)

ANGIE (*sings*): Hark! the herald angels sing,
Glory to the newborn King;
Peace on earth, and mercy mild,

> *God and sinners reconciled!*
> *Joyful all ye nations rise,*
> *Join the triumph of the skies;*
> *With th' angelic host proclaim*
> *Christ is born in Bethlehem.*

(*As she sings, the trumpet sounds again. The hoofbeats grow. The blast gets louder. Prison bars start to collapse. All of the bars fall out of the walls, collapse to the floor with a great noise. Women step slowly out of their cells. A helicopter sounds in the background. Everyone sits quietly. No one knows what to say.*)

ANGIE: What more do you need?

SHARON: Get out of here.

(ANGIE *leaves.* SHARON *is alone in the cell.*

FOSTER *walks down the corridor.*)

SHARON: What are you doing here?

FOSTER: I want to know what happens next.

SHARON: Are you scared?

FOSTER: I don't know. I never had any faith. But you did.

SHARON: Yep.

FOSTER: So?

SHARON: So.

FOSTER: Well, if the world is coming to an end, this isn't the place to be. Let's go.

EXTERIOR: ROAD. DAY.

SHARON *rides behind* FOSTER *on his motorcycle.*

Hoofbeats are closer. The red horse ridden by a rider wielding a long sword chases them. The rider holds a pair of scales. The trumpet continues to sound.

Cut to:

EXTERIOR: THE ROAD. NIGHT.

SHARON *and* FOSTER *are on the bike. The night sky is filled with the image of a huge bull ridden by a ghostly woman holding an immense candelabra.*

Cut to:

* * *

EXTERIOR: FARTHER DOWN THE ROAD. DUSK.

The motorcycle comes to the crest of a hill.
Smoke surrounds the two. It is impossible to go ahead. They stop driv-
ing. The smoke obscures everything now. Hoofbeats. The world is
dissolving. The FOURTH HORSEMAN, DEATH, *riding the pale horse, ap-*
pears in the fog of smoke and comes slowly toward them.
SHARON *and* FOSTER *get off their motorbike and watch the horseman.*
Then, they begin to rise slowly into the smoke. She doesn't want this.

SHARON: No! No, I don't want to go. (*To* FOSTER:) Don't let
me go. No!

(*They disappear into the smoke.*
Dissolve to:)

EXTERIOR: LIMBO. NIGHT.

We are in the dark. The noise has stopped. Then we see them, barely
lit, a hint of something like moonlight on them. A voice, Mary's:

MARY: Mom? (MARY *walks out of the darkness. She is be-*
side them, holding her panda.) Hi, Mom.

FOSTER: Is this Hell?

SHARON (*tenderly*): Hello, Mary.

(SHARON *walks to her, but* MARY *is just out of reach and stays there.*)

FOSTER: That's your daughter.

SHARON: Mary? Where are you?

MARY: I'm here.

SHARON: Where are we?

MARY: You know when you hear those songs about the
river that washes away all your sins? Well, here it is.
Heaven is on the other side of the river.

FOSTER: We're in Heaven. Why are we in Heaven?

MARY: You're not in Heaven. Heaven is over there.

(*She points to the distance, into the darkness.*)

FOSTER: I can't see it.

MARY: It's there. If you love God, it's there. Foster. Do you
love God for giving you the gift of life?

FOSTER (*whispers*): Yes.

(Then he smiles, and then he disappears.)

SHARON: No!

MARY: Mommy! Gabriel is coming. You have to make up your mind.

SHARON: There's nothing more to say. Take me to God, Mary. I have to speak to Him.

MARY: You have to love God.

SHARON: I love you, Mary.

MARY: That isn't enough.

SHARON: Baby, it's all I have. If life is a gift, if it really is a gift, and there really is a Heaven . . .

MARY: There really is a Heaven.

SHARON: Then why should I thank Him for the gift of so much suffering, Mary, so much pain on the Earth that He created. Let me ask Him why?

MARY: Tell God you love Him.

SHARON: I can't.

MARY: If you don't tell God that you love Him, you can't go to Heaven. Tell God that you love Him. Mommy!

SHARON: No.

(And then we hear Gabriel's final call. Gabriel's melody is like the infinite regression of an image in parallel mirrors, and the melody stretches into the end of time. While they listen, a gold light, as though a sun is setting, fills Sharon's face. MARY takes her hand and stands beside her. The gold light shines on both of them.)

MARY: Do you see Heaven?

SHARON: Yes.

MARY: Isn't it beautiful?

SHARON: Yes.

(MARY lets go of SHARON.)

MARY: Do you know how long you have to stay here?

SHARON: Yes.

(MARY fades away.)

MARY: How long?

(And to the darkness, SHARON says:)

SHARON: Forever.

(She is alone. We pull back.)

The Rapture

(Original Draft)

The rest of mankind who survived these plagues still did not abjure the gods their hands had fashioned, nor cease their worship of devils and of idols made from gold, silver, bronze, stone, and wood, which cannot see or hear or walk. Nor did they repent of their murders, their sorcery, their fornication, or their robberies.

Revelation 9:20–21

If a man is on the roof, he must not come down to fetch his goods from the house; if in the field, he must not turn back for his coat.

Matthew 24:17

It will be a time of great distress; there has never been such a time from the beginning of the world until now, and will never be again.

Matthew 24:21

But her child was snatched up to God and his throne; and the woman herself fled into the wilds, where she had a place prepared for her by God.

Revelation 12:5–6

INTERIOR: LIVING ROOM. NIGHT.

The music is slow, but the two couples in the room are dancing behind the beat, holding close, grinding together. It is late at night, a casual, friendly hour. The two couples are good-looking Americans, rock-and-roll fans who lift their lighters overhead at the end of the festival, who drive pickups that are raised above the wheels. They are long haired, sharp featured, ignorant of sin.

One of the men reaches to the woman with the other man, and pulls her face to his. They kiss. The couples separate, and the kissers embrace while the other two watch for a moment; then they too begin to make out. The other man and woman unbutton each other's shirts. The only person who concerns us in the room is the woman of the first kiss, SHARON.

The music stops. The couples stop for a moment and look at each other, waiting for the next move. For a second, they are shy.
Cut to:

INTERIOR: BEDROOM. NIGHT.

SHARON *sits on the edge of a large water bed, smoking a cigarette. Behind her in the bed are the other three people, asleep.* SHARON *looks numb, horrified, lost.*
Cut to:

EXTERIOR: A HIGHWAY IN THE SIERRAS. DAY.

SHARON *drives, smoking a cigarette. She still has a sad look. She has come to the country for solace, to figure something out, but the answer hasn't appeared. She can barely phrase the question.*
Cut to:

* * *

INTERIOR: MOTEL ROOM. DAY.

SHARON *pulls the drapes closed against the lovely view. She sits in the middle of the bed; she is frozen with indecision.*

She reaches for her bag. She opens it. She takes out: a small pistol, a pint of vodka, a handful of red pills.

She swallows a pill with the vodka. She puts the gun to her forehead, closes her eyes, and holds the gun for a long moment. She opens her eyes.

The disorder of the room bothers her. She straightens out the bed, puts everything from the bag but the gun back into it, and then the dirty ashtray on the night table bothers her. She pulls the drawer open to hide the ashtray, and she finds the Gideon Bible. She puts the ashtray on top of the Bible and closes the drawer.

She sits with the gun in her hand and stares at it. She puts the gun down, a bit disgusted with herself, disappointed at her lack of resolve. She lights another cigarette and looks for the ashtray. She opens the night-table drawer and takes the ashtray off the Bible. Then she takes the Bible out of the drawer and opens it.

SHARON *starts to read the Bible, toward the back of the book, from the New Testament.*

Day turns to night.

A blinding light fills the room. SHARON *is thrown backward by it, and before she's eclipsed by brilliance, we see her weeping and covering her eyes.*

Fade-out:

Fade-in:

EXTERIOR: ZOO. DAY.

A few years later. SHARON *is with her new* HUSBAND *and two children,* JAMES, *about five, and* MARY, *three or four.* SHARON *wears a T-shirt that says* Christians Aren't Perfect, Just Forgiven. *Her hair is shorter. She wears a cross around her neck. Her belt buckle is the fish symbol.* SHARON *is happy. She loves her* HUSBAND *and he loves her.*

Cut to:

* * *

EXTERIOR: TRAILER PARK. DAY.

The trailer park sits on the edge of an orange grove. SHARON *is at the window of a mobile home, looking out at the grove. The grove and the park are old neighbors; you get the feeling both are doomed. The children play in the kitchen behind* SHARON.
Cut to:

EXTERIOR: ORANGE GROVE. DAY.

A group, say, four or five African men, stroll through the grove, singing. Their song is passionate, the harmonies suggest tribe; the melody suggests radio. They pass near the trailer park.

EXTERIOR: SHARON'S TRAILER. DAY.

SHARON, *at the window, is captivated by the song and disturbed by it. She leaves the window.*

EXTERIOR: ORANGE GROVE. DAY.

The men sit and are quiet. SHARON *climbs through a hole in the fence. She studies the Africans carefully, cautiously. The Africans watch* SHARON *as though she were a movie or far away.*

SHARON: I've been waiting for a sign, and I heard your song, and now I know. All my life, I've had the feeling that something was waiting for me. And I always knew that when it happened, I would recognize it and that I wouldn't mistake it for something else. Like I wouldn't have something happen to me, and I would say this is it! and then later say, no, that wasn't it. It was a secret feeling, and I never told anyone about it. (*She stops and measures the moment.*) Even when I found God, I knew that there was something more. You're Angels of Death, aren't you? When I heard you singing, I knew that you'd come to tell me that these are the last days. I always knew it would come to me through music. (*Another pause.*) Even a lot of people who say they're believers don't really believe that these are the last days, but I do, I know they are. Even the ones who say that your credit card number is the mark of the Beast, or that the United Nations is the Whore of Babylon prophesied by Revelation and Daniel, they don't really believe. But these are the Days of the Tribulations, the First Tribulations, the seals have been broken, the book will be opened, the Day of Rapture is approaching. I'm not afraid. I accepted Jesus as my personal savior five years ago. But I guess you know that. We'll be taken bodily into the air, bodily into Heaven, and we'll be moved into homes that Jesus is building for us right now, and even if it is only temporary housing, while Armageddon is fought on Earth, it will still be Paradise, until God's Kingdom is established back on Earth, until the mansions have been built. Can I kiss you? I feel so much love for you right now. Is it love or is it gratitude? Can't gratitude be a kind of prayer? If you give thanks to the Lord, isn't that ultimate gratitude an expression of ultimate love, the love of the children for the Father? These are the last days, and soon Jesus will be taking us bodily into Heaven, and it will be peaceful for a thousand years. So, can I kiss you?

(*Maybe the Africans are couriers from God. Maybe they are refugees. Maybe they are a soccer team or students. Maybe they speak English; maybe they don't. She kisses each African on the forehead.*
SHARON *goes back to her trailer. She feels blessed, full of grace.*
Cut to:*)

EXTERIOR: TRAILER PARK. NIGHT.
SHARON *sits outside the trailer, talking to a friend,* SUSAN, *while* SHARON'S HUSBAND *sips beer and watches* JAMES *and* MARY. *Dinner is over, and the families in the park are relaxed. Occasionally,* SHARON *and her* HUSBAND *exchange silent, warm glances.*

SUSAN: Sharon, if I'm ironing Bill's shirts, and the Lord calls me into Heaven, if the Day of Rapture has arrived,

and I'm taken away from the ironing board, will the iron
scorch what's left on the board?

(*Another woman,* PAULA, *sticks her head out of a trailer window.
She's the local skeptic.*)

PAULA: Does the iron have a Teflon base?

(SHARON *and* SUSAN *ignore her.*)

SHARON: Bill still won't accept the Lord.

SUSAN: No.

SHARON: Maybe we should talk about that for a minute.

SUSAN: Maybe we should talk about that for an hour. He
says he believes in the Lord in his own way.

SHARON: But he doesn't accept Jesus as his personal
savior.

SUSAN (*smiling*): Maybe I better get him some shirts that
are permanent press.

SHARON: We know that God sees every sparrow fall,
but, sparrows or irons, He's not obliged to pick them
up.

PAULA: Sharon, could you answer a question? Okay, the
Rapture is happening, right? Prophecy is coming true, the
whole ball of wax. As it is written, right? Now. Do you
ascend bodily through the roof of the car, or spiritually
through it, or does the car stop, so you have a chance to
powder your nose before you meet your Maker? Also,
what happens to the food that's in your stomach? Are
there bathrooms in Heaven?

SHARON: I think you're making fun of me. I think the
answer is in your heart.

PAULA: Well, you see these people with their bumper
stickers that say, Warning, in Case of Rapture This Car
Will Be Unmanned. So God is going to just yank Christian
drivers out of their cars during rush hour, if that's when
He returns? There'd be accidents. Do you think God
wants to cause accidents?

SHARON: God wants to warn people as dramatically as
possible that He is coming back. And a traffic accident at
rush hour is nothing compared to eternal Hell.

PAULA (*saving the tense moment*): Well, maybe I'll get a convertible or keep the sunroof open all the time. (*Catches Sharon's grin.*) Wait, wait, is that a smile? Calling Satan, calling Satan, I got one for you.

SHARON: Paula, just think about it, not for me but for you.

JAMES: I'm sleepy.

SHARON'S HUSBAND: Well, if it's your bedtime, then it's my bedtime.

(*Cut to:*)

EXTERIOR: CONSTRUCTION SITE. DAY.
Sharon's HUSBAND, *killed by falling equipment, is lifted by co-workers out of a pile of wreckage.*
Cut to:

EXTERIOR: TRAILER PARK. NIGHT.
A crowd stands hushed outside Sharon's trailer.
Cut to:

EXTERIOR: CEMETERY. DAY.
SHARON *and the children, followed by friends, walk away from the grave.*
Cut to:

EXTERIOR: TRAILER. DAY.
SHARON *stands at the door, talking to the trailer park* MANAGER.

MANAGER: Now, if I hear that you're worrying about paying this month's rent, then I'm going to charge you double. You know what I'm saying?

(SHARON *smiles.*)

MANAGER: You have to start looking for a job, right?

(SHARON *nods her head. It's hard for her to talk.*)

MANAGER: Wrong.

(*Cut to:*)

* * *

INTERIOR: PHOTOLAB. DAY.

Extreme close-up of color snapshots gliding in front of us. When an out-of-focus picture passes by, a hand enters the frame and marks an X on it with a red pen.

Pull back to reveal:

SHARON *checks the print quality in a 50-Minute Photolab; she is at the printing machine, which sits in the window, in a small shopping plaza. She wears a white lab coat. The modern family passes under her eyes. In a few pictures, we see her* HUSBAND *wearing the clothes he died in, and he is trying to reach her, to say something to her.* SHARON *accepts his place in the pictures, in the scheme of things.*

Landscapes. Birthday parties. A naked couple posed seductively for a swingers' magazine. SHARON *closes her eyes.*

Cut to:

INTERIOR: TRAILER. NIGHT.

SHARON *tucks the children into bed. She goes into her room and kneels before a small shrine. She prays. Her face fills with light. When the light subsides, she smiles peacefully. The vision has given her a mission.*

Cut to:

INTERIOR: PHOTOLAB. DAY.

More pictures of America. Her HUSBAND *appears in improbable settings: at pool parties, graduations, Disneyland. Now he is waving to* SHARON *as though he can see her across a river, as though he has just made her out in a crowd.*

Cut to:

EXTERIOR: TRAILER PARK. DAY.

The MANAGER *inspects Sharon's trailer closely. He is doing something he doesn't want to do, and he is worried about* SHARON.

MANAGER: All right, all right . . . I'll give you fifty-five hundred dollars.

SHARON: You know it isn't worth that much.

PAULA: Fine, I'll give you ten dollars. Now you can't afford to leave. (PAULA, *the skeptic, is hysterical because* SHARON *wants to leave.*) Sharon! What in the name of God are you doing? This is your home. You don't leave your home. You don't leave your friends. Where the hell are you going?

SHARON: Someplace better, for the children.

PAULA: Where?

SHARON: Get a convertible. Keep the top down.

(*Cut to:*)

EXTERIOR: RIVERSIDE COUNTY. DAY.

SHARON *and the children, in a convertible, are driving toward the desert.*

Cut to:

INTERIOR: GAS STATION MINIMART. NIGHT.

We're in the high desert now, Twenty-nine Palms. SHARON *pays for gas and after receiving her change, puts it in the collection container for the Jerry Lewis Telethon. No one watches her. She takes a wad of bills from her bag, the money she got for the trailer, pries the lid off the collection cup, stuffs the money in, replaces the lid, and leaves.*

Cut to:

EXTERIOR: JOSHUA TREE CAMPGROUND. DAY.

SHARON *and her children have made an incongruous home in a campsite wedged between the weird rocks.* JAMES *colors in a Christian coloring book.* MARY *rides a tricycle.* SHARON *makes hot chocolate on a Coleman stove.*

A strange siren starts suddenly, loudly. SHARON *looks to the sky, then runs for the children, grabbing their hands. She pulls them with her as she climbs one of the great stone hills.*

At the top, she stands up, with Mary *in her arm and* James *holding her hand. She looks like a monument to motherhood, to prepared-ness, to anticipation. The wind ruffles her hair. The siren contin-ues for a moment, and we can see, from this vantage point, down to the campground. A rock climber (wearing the gear) runs to a Saab, swearing, opens the door, and turns off the alarm. The siren stops.*

Sharon, *troubled, starts back down the rocks.*

EXTERIOR: JOSHUA TREE CAMPGROUND. NIGHT.

A park ranger, Terry Nelson *(she wears a brass name tag on her shirt), drives into the campground. She stops at Sharon's car and watches for a moment. Sharon's trunk is open, filled with dehy-drated food and water.* Terry *walks to where* Sharon *and the chil-dren are having dinner by the light of a kerosene lantern.*

Terry: Howdy.

Sharon: Hi.

Terry: Is everything okay?

Sharon (*a little guilty*): We've been here too long, haven't we? We're not supposed to stay longer than two weeks, I know. I'm sorry. I thought we'd be leaving sooner.

Terry: Oh well, things are sort of slack now. Most people won't hit the road for a month or so. Where are you from?

Sharon: Fontana.

Terry: Lost your job?

Sharon: I quit.

Terry: What are you doing in Joshua Tree?

Sharon (*indicates*): There's nothing overhead.

Terry: You haven't been down the hill for food or water.

Sharon: We have enough left.

Terry: Left until when?

Sharon: Until He returns.

Terry: Your husband?

Sharon: The Son of God.

(*Cut to:*)

*   *   *

EXTERIOR: ANOTHER AREA IN JOSHUA TREE. DAY.
SHARON *and the children wander aimlessly on the paths and over the rocks. The children have begun looking to the sky, like hitchhikers by an empty highway, scanning the road for traffic.*
Cut to:

EXTERIOR: CAMPSITE. NIGHT.
The trunk of the car is open. SHARON *looks through the empty cardboard boxes for food. There is none. Her last water bottle is almost empty. She looks at the children, who are bored and fighting with each other.*
Cut to:

EXTERIOR: THE DESERT. NIGHT.
SHARON *and the children leave the park, heading down the hill toward Twenty-nine Palms.*

EXTERIOR: BURGER KING. NIGHT.
Sharon's car is at the drive-up window. A bag of food is waiting for her.
   BURGER KING WORKER: That's six-eighty.
(SHARON *fumbles with her purse.*)
   JAMES (*confidentially, to* MARY): Mommy doesn't have any
      money.
(*The* BURGER KING WORKER *holds the bag in his hand.* SHARON *reaches up and grabs it, then drives away.*)
   BURGER KING WORKER (*to* OTHER WORKER): Call the police.
   OTHER WORKER: Forget about it.
   BURGER KING WORKER: I'm not paying for her dinner.
(*Cut to:*)

INTERIOR: CAR. NIGHT.
SHARON *returns to Joshua Tree. The children are devouring their burgers and fries.*

* * *

EXTERIOR: CAR. NIGHT.

The car drives into a parking lot designated No Overnight Camping.

EXTERIOR: JOSHUA TREE. NIGHT.

It is a dark night with a thin, unromantic sliver of moon. There are stars, but the rocks, which we can see only as negative space, cut out most of the sky.

The children kneel, praying. SHARON *stands behind them.*

SHARON: Do you love me?

JAMES: Yes.

SHARON: James, do you love Jesus?

JAMES: Yes.

SHARON: Do you believe in Heaven?

JAMES: Yes.

SHARON: You know in Heaven there's Jesus and Baby Jesus, together, and Baby Jesus has the special job of watching out for all the children. Mary, do you love Baby Jesus?

MARY: Yes.

SHARON: It's not fair to make you pay because I'm lost. Nothing in Heaven is broken. I love you.

(*Now we see the gun. She pulls the trigger and shoots* JAMES *in the head. At the explosion, we have an extreme close-up of Mary's shocked face.*

SHARON *pulls the trigger again, but the gun doesn't fire.*)

SHARON: Mary, do you love Baby Jesus?

MARY: Yes.

(MARY *makes a face as though she's about to enter icy water. She clasps her hands in prayer even harder.*)

SHARON: Tell Him that. Don't be afraid.

(SHARON *pulls the trigger and the gun fires.* MARY *is dead.*

Fade-out:

Fade-in:)

* * *

EXTERIOR: JOSHUA TREE. LATER.

SHARON *walks away from two small graves, carrying a shovel. She had expected to feel joy that they were with God, but instead she feels empty.*
Cut to:

INTERIOR: COCKTAIL LOUNGE. NIGHT.

Some time has passed, a week? Longer? SHARON *sits alone at the bar, drinking. A* GUY *sees her, studies her, makes his move.*

GUY: Hey, pretty lady.

(SHARON *takes the gun from her bag and jams it against the bridge of the guy's nose.*)

SHARON: Why don't you talk to someone else?

(*Cut to:*)

EXTERIOR: THE MIDDLE OF NOWHERE. NIGHT.

SHARON *drives. She's speeding. The red lights of a highway patrol car appear behind her. The siren is close. She is sure she has been caught. She pulls over.*

The highway patrolman, OFFICER FOSTER, *gets out of his car and shines his searchlight on Sharon's car.*

FOSTER (*through a loudspeaker*): Get out of the car, please. Slowly.

(SHARON *gets out of the car and stares into the light, not shielding her eyes, even enjoying the glare, taking it as a small dose of punishment. She wants to blink but resists.*)

FOSTER (*still through the speaker though they are ten feet apart*): Now your driver's license and registration, please.

(SHARON *indicates she has to get them from her car. Inside the car, she considers the gun, then rejects it, gets her papers, and gets out of the car. She holds the license and registration out in her hand.*)

FOSTER: Thank you.

(*He walks to* SHARON, *takes the identification, and goes back to his car.*)

FOSTER: Is the car yours?
(SHARON *nods yes.*
He studies her driver's license.)
   FOSTER: Sharon? . . . Do you know that you were going
   faster than a hundred miles an hour?
(*We look at* FOSTER *for a moment. He is not a bad man, and he is
studying* SHARON, *less as another speeder than as a woman in obvi-
ous trouble.*)
   FOSTER: You're not drunk.
(SHARON *isn't, and she shakes her head no. She can't tell if she wants
to be arrested for killing her children, or if she wants to get away, or
even if she wants to kill* FOSTER.)
   FOSTER: Sharon, is there anything you want to talk about?
(*He seems sincere, and even if he is aware of sex, he also wants to
satisfy his curiosity.* SHARON *allows herself a trace of a weary smile,
because she knows so much more than he does.*)
   SHARON: Do you believe in God?
   FOSTER (*answers her seriously*): Not anymore.
(SHARON *takes the cross from around her neck and holds it up. The
cross gleams in the light.*)
   SHARON: What does this mean?
   FOSTER: You tell me.
   SHARON: Where do you live?
(*As far as* SHARON *is concerned, she is damned. What does she have
to lose now? She drops the cross.*
Cut to:)

EXTERIOR: FOSTER'S HOUSE. DAY.
It is late afternoon. SHARON *and* FOSTER *live together. They may even
be married. They are having a party, and the guests are dressed well:
it could be an anniversary. Everyone moves slowly.* SHARON *and* FOS-
TER *stand near the fence, facing the desert, away from the party.*
FOSTER *is troubled.*
   FOSTER: I know what you want to say to me. You want to
   say, "You think you know me, but you don't know me."
   SHARON: What do you think you know?

FOSTER: That you won't stay with me forever.

(SHARON *doesn't say anything.*)

FOSTER: To which you say, "That's a long time."

SHARON: What else do I say?

FOSTER: That you can't promise me anything. I could ask you why you're so quiet, but I know the answer to that, too.

SHARON: How do I answer?

FOSTER: You say that you said it all a long time ago. But you didn't say it to me.

SHARON: I'm going for a walk.

FOSTER: Will you come back?

SHARON: Do you want me to?

FOSTER: If you think I love you.

(*He walks back to his house, to the guests.* SHARON *strolls into the desert.*

There's a feeling that a little time has passed. The light changes; it is dark now. SHARON *stops far enough from the house so that the light it casts falls short of her.*

A flaming sword slices the air between SHARON *and us; and as we shift position, we see the sword is held by the* ARCHANGEL MICHAEL.

Another angel drifts into the scene; and when her billowing robe settles, it becomes a curtain that holds the projected images of JAMES *and* MARY, *dressed as they were when they died, still dirty from the grave, and pale. Photographed from below, they seem to float and look down like cherubim painted on a ceiling fresco.*)

JAMES (*sincerely, with a little difficulty*): Jesus is coming back, Mommy. There are wars and rumors of wars, Mommy, and a curse devours the Earth, and those who live in it are held guilty.

MARY: Don't be sorry that you killed us, Mommy, it doesn't matter that you killed us, because we're happy now.

JAMES: Mother, listen to me. This is the end of history. The living outnumber the dead. The Armies of the Lord are waiting for the Day of Judgement. Do you still love Jesus, Mommy?

SHARON: What if I say no?

MARY: Don't say no, Mommy.

JAMES: The only one who should fear is the one who has rejected God's gracious offer of forgiveness and pardon that was paid for by the death of God's Son.

SHARON: How can I love a God who let me kill my children?

MARY: Jesus loves you because you love Him.

SHARON: Why?

JAMES: I know you want us back, but we can't come back, Mommy. We're dead.

(*James's attention is drawn to something we can't see. He disappears for a moment. When he returns, he has a baby in his arms, an infant boy, naked.*)

MARY: Look, Mommy, Baby Jesus.

(*The* ARCHANGEL MICHAEL *swings his sword, and the vision disappears. The other angel withdraws into the darkness, and then* MICHAEL, *too, is gone.*

SHARON *starts to walk to the house. When she passes a twisted cactus, it shines suddenly with Christmas lights. She passes another cactus, which lights up, and then a third, and a fourth.*
Cut to:)

INTERIOR: HOUSE. NIGHT.

The party continues. FOSTER *watches* SHARON *cross the lawn. She comes into the house.*

FOSTER: What happens now?

(*She smiles the way she smiled when he stopped her for speeding. Then she raises a hand and points to the sky. We hear a trumpet playing one long, extended note.*
The party guests look outside to the apparent source of the music.
A MAN *turns on the radio. The trumpet is across the entire band.*)

MAN: It's the Archangel Gabriel blowing his trumpet.

FOSTER: It's a military test. There's secret military installations spread out over the high desert, and this is some kind of test.

(*The* MAN *has turned on the television. He changes the channel, but the picture is always the same: a long trumpet raised high before a deep blue background. A hand holds the trumpet, but we don't see the angel.*)

WOMAN: It's God. He's giving us a chance to save ourselves.

ANOTHER GUEST: It's the Russians.

ANOTHER WOMAN (*sarcastic*): Right. It's a practical joke from the godless Communists.. And we'll retaliate by dropping a pie on the Kremlin. Right. The Russians.

(*The* GUEST *didn't really believe it: it was more of a wish. Everyone stares at the set, except* SHARON. FOSTER *watches her. He seems unimpressed with the miracle, if that is what it is.*

The trumpet stops. It disappears from the screen and is replaced with a new image: a lamb with seven eyes. A WOMAN *turns off the television. Her* HUSBAND *puts his arm around her.*)

WOMAN'S HUSBAND: There should be six more blasts of the trumpet. You have until the last call to . . . repent.

WOMAN: I guess we should all pray.

ANOTHER WOMAN: Would it bother anyone if I sang?

(*There's no objection, and for a moment, she's stuck; impulse has preceded selection. She finds the right music.*)

ANOTHER WOMAN (*sings*): *Hark! the herald angels sing*
Glory to the newborn King . . .

(SHARON *has left the room.* FOSTER *looks for her. She has gone to the garage.*)

INTERIOR: GARAGE. NIGHT.

SHARON *is on a motorcycle. The garage door is open.* FOSTER *comes into the garage just as she starts the bike up. When he approaches her, the trumpet sounds a second time. They stare at each other through the blast. He reaches into his jacket and takes a photograph from a pocket. He offers it to her. It is a picture of* SHARON *with the children. Stamped across the snapshot is* WANTED FOR MURDER.

FOSTER: This came in today.

(*The trumpet stops. We hear hoofbeats. The* FOUR HORSEMEN OF THE

APOCALYPSE *ride past the house. First, the white horse passes, and his rider holds a bow and arrow.*

    FOSTER: Sharon, where are you going?

    SHARON: What if there was no God? What if I had killed my children, and there was no God?

(*The* SECOND HORSEMAN *rides by: a red horse, the rider wielding a sword.*)

    FOSTER: Where are you going?

    SHARON: Don't you know? I'm going to Hell.

    FOSTER: You can save yourself.

    SHARON: I want to suffer eternal damnation. I want to burn in a fire which will be as painful after a million years as it will be when the demons first throw me into the pit.

(*The* THIRD HORSEMAN *appears: a black horse, the rider carrying a pair of scales.*)

    FOSTER: I'm coming with you.

(*The* FOURTH HORSEMAN: *the pale horse ridden by* DEATH.)

    SHARON: Why?

    FOSTER: I love you.

(*Cut to:*)

EXTERIOR: THE ROAD. DAY.

Another blast of the trumpet. SHARON *on one motorcycle and* FOSTER *on his own pass a cluster of the faithful standing beside their cars, looking up to the sky, waiting for the end.*

Cut to:

EXTERIOR: A SMALL TOWN. DAY.

A store is being looted. SHARON *and* FOSTER *watch as a few unbelievers break windows. The cash register is hurled through a window. When it lands, it explodes with money.* SHARON *watches a couple fucking behind a counter.* FOSTER *takes as a souvenir a coin from the cash register. The trumpet sounds again.*

Cut to:

* * *

EXTERIOR: THE ROAD. DAY.

SHARON *and* FOSTER *ride behind a convertible. The trumpet sounds again, the fifth call.* FOSTER *holds up a hand, the fingers spread.*
The driver of the convertible lifts out of the car and zooms up into the sky.
The car, out of control, swerves off the road and drifts to a stop in the chaparral.
SHARON *speeds up.* FOSTER *follows, staying a bit in back of her. The trumpet sounds again, the sixth call.*
The two motorcycles come to the crest of a hill and look down on a small community. People are rising into the sky quickly, faster than bubbles in water.
Red smoke begins to surround the two. They stop driving. The smoke obscures everything now, and small fires seem to be starting all over the ground.
The world is dissolving.
SHARON *begins to rise slowly from the motorcycle. She doesn't want this.*

>SHARON: No! Put me down, I don't want to go. (*To* FOS-
>TER:) Hold my hand, don't let me go.

(He reaches up, grabs her hand, and then he too is rising with her. They disappear into the smoke.
Cut to:)

EXTERIOR: PARADISE. DAY.

SHARON *and* FOSTER *stand on the bank of a gentle river. It looks like the lower Colorado; the green shore yields quickly to the desert.*
People, families, walk along the far shore.
JAMES *and* MARY, *in a small rowboat, are just a few yards from* SHARON *and* FOSTER.

>MARY (*to* FOSTER): What do you have in your hand?
(He holds up the coin from the cash register.)
>JAMES: You're only here because my mother invited you.
>You have to go to Hell now.

(FOSTER *is gone. A small fire burns where he stood.*)

    JAMES: God sees into your heart, and He knows that you
    love Him. All you have to do is admit it to yourself.

    SHARON: I love you. Isn't that enough?

    MARY: No.

    JAMES: Gabriel is coming, Mom, you have to make up
    your mind.

(*The* ARCHANGEL GABRIEL *stands in the bow of a long and narrow
boat, a gold horn in his hands. He puts it to his lips, and then we
hear the seventh call.*

*In Brahms's First Symphony, just before the introduction of the
fourth movement theme, there is a horn solo, French horn, I think.
Gabriel's melody sounds something like that, but it seems to come,
though not on every note, from more than one instrument. It's like
the infinite regression of an image in parallel mirrors, stretching the
melody into the end of time.*

*The call is over. Where the wake from the Archangel's passing boat
laps against the riverbank, people are rising from the water.*

SHARON *finally seems filled with grace, finally looks peaceful.*

Her children are rowing away from her. MARY *sees someone across
the river.*)

    SHARON: Come back. Take me to God. I have to say I'm
    sorry.

    JAMES: It's too late.

    MARY: Look! There's Daddy.

(SHARON'S HUSBAND *stands on the other shore, quiet, sad.*)

    SHARON: Too late?

    JAMES: Yeah. You had to say it before Gabriel's final call.
    It's over.

    MARY: Daddy! Daddy!

    SHARON: But what happens to me now?

    JAMES: You have to stay where you are.

    SHARON: For how long?

    JAMES (*amazed that she still doesn't get it*): Forever.

(*He rows toward his father.*)

The New Age

Filmmakers

Written and Directed by	Michael Tolkin
Executive Producer	Oliver Stone
Executive Producer	Arnon Milchan
Producer	Nick Wechsler
Producer	Keith Addis
Co-Producer	Iya Labunka
Co-Producer	Janet Yang
Director of Photography	John Campbell
Editor	Suzanne Fenn
Production Designer	Robin Standefer
Music by	Mark Mothersbaugh
Costume Designer	Richard Shissler
Casting	Deborah Aquila, C.S.A.

Cast

Peter Witner	Peter Weller
Katherine Witner	Judy Davis
Jean Levy	Patrick Bauchau
Sarah Friedberg	Rachel Rosenthal

Jeff Witner	Adam West
Alison Gale	Paula Marshall
Misha	Bruce Ramsay
Bettina	Tanya Pohlkotte
Ellen Saltonstall	Susan Traylor
Anna	Patricia Heaton
Lyle	John Diehl
Laura	Maureen Mueller
Mary Netter	Sandra Seacat
Dale Deveaux	Samuel L. Jackson
Sandi Rego	Audra Lindley
Kevin Bulasky	Corbin Bernsen
Paul Hartmann	Jonathan Hadary
Sue	Lily Mariye
Other Katherine	Kimberley Kates
Hilly	Maria Ellingsen
Carol	Kelly Miller
Emily	Dana Hollowell
Woman Customer	Rebecca Staab
Man Customer	Alexander Pourtash
Swimmer	Scott Layne
Tina Bulasky	Mary Kane
Chet	Patrick Dollaghan
Tab	Jeff Weston
Nova Trainee	Lisa Pescia
Victoria	Victoria Baker
Bob	Bob Flanagan
Rich German	Nicole Nagel
Andrea	Dana Kaminski
Pagan Woman	Cheri Gaulke

TITLE SEQUENCE 1
Fade-in:

INTERIOR: YOGA STUDIO. DAY.
A white screen. We don't know how far away it is until a wo-
man crosses the frame in close-up. Her accent is hard to
place: Europe, but a long time ago. Her name is SARAH. *Time*
dissolving.

> SARAH FRIEDBERG (*voice-over*): Sit up straight with your
> feet on the floor and expand your back. The first thing
> you need to do is to feel the Earth's power under your
> feet. And then your seat, feel how you're sitting. And then
> your back. Keep your neck relaxed, your shoulders
> down, and without forcing anything, feel the crown of
> your head reaching for the sky. And now observe your
> breath, watch your breath as though you are watching
> someone else. Then watch your thoughts as though you
> are watching someone else. And don't chase away any
> images that come to you, just watch them . . .

(She pulls down a screen. Blackness.
Cut to:)

TITLE SEQUENCE 2
Cut to:

INTERIOR: KATHERINE'S OFFICE. DAY.
KATHERINE WITNER, *a graphic designer, is on the phone with her client*
at the bank, BARRY. KATHERINE *is very upset.*

KATHERINE: No, no. What! What?

(*Samples of a bank's logo are all over the office: on brochures, T-shirts, letterheads. Her Asian assistant,* SUE, *is with her discussing prices with a printer.*)

SUE: It's twenty weight . . . coated . . .

KATHERINE: Barry, what are you saying? But Barry . . . Barry . . . you owe me thirty-eight thousand dollars! Barry, Barry . . . you promised me that money, Well, thank you, Barry. Good-bye, Barry.

(*She's just at that point where the loss of youth, and the possibilities it held for her, leaves her frightened, and the cost of the denial of that fear shows in her eyes. Very calmly and deliberately,* KATHERINE *starts to erase all the files on her computer.*)

SUE: What did Barry say?

KATHERINE: Barry was fired.

SUE: Wow, too bad, I like Barry.

(KATHERINE *quietly drags her mouse and begins to erase all of her bank files.*)

SUE: Katherine, what are you doing?

(*Close on the Macintosh screen. Wiping out the files is like a video game. She drags the files to the trash-can icon, which has been programmed to make elaborate explosion sounds, as the computer asks her:* THE TRASH CONTAINS 72 ITEMS. IT USES 10 MG OF SPACE, ARE YOU SURE YOU WANT TO PERMANENTLY REMOVE IT? *She is.*)

SUE: Katherine, you're erasing all the files. Wait, we haven't backed up these files yet! Katherine, you're destroying your work.

KATHERINE (*while she's erasing*): The bank doesn't need a hundred thousand brochures because the bank doesn't exist anymore. The bank doesn't exist anymore because too many of its big real estate loans went bad. Its great big real estate loans went bad because it made loans for shopping centers that can't find enough tenants. The shopping centers can't find enough tenants because there are too many shopping centers. There are too many shopping centers because a lot of greedy fucks got loans from corrupt banks.

SUE: What are you going to do?

KATHERINE: I'm going shopping.

(*The computer's screen saver takes over: flying toasters.*
Cut to:)

TITLE SEQUENCE 3
Cut to:

INTERIOR: CLOTHING STORE. DAY.

A serious ritual: trying on clothes in a fashionable boutique. The
careful examination of the image in the mirror. PETER WITNER. PETER
is a little too charming, a little too glib. His style is not Armani, not so
serious; he is trendier than that, more clever. Right now, he's trying
on jackets, and he is shopping with his father, JEFF WITNER, *a silver*
fox, in his sixties, with an eye tuck and a hair transplant. HILLY, *a*
saleswoman, is with them. Everyone is focused on JEFF *and the jacket*
he has tried on. Also watching them is CAROL, *Jeff's thirty-year-old*
girlfriend du jour.

PETER: Dad?

JEFF: Did I ask for your opinion yet? Carol?

CAROL (*afraid to tell him her opinion*): It's okay.

JEFF: Hilly?

HILLY: Hmmm.

(*A look from* PETER.)

HILLY: No. It doesn't work.

JEFF: You don't think so? Or Peter doesn't want you to
think so?

PETER: Dad, it's very . . . uh . . . how do I say this politely,
it's . . . working a little too hard . . . it's, how do I say
this . . .

JEFF: Say it!

PETER: You look too much like a Del Taco–franchise
owner who lives in Palm Springs, goes to the mall, walks
into one of those stores for guys who cruise the disco in
the Holiday Inn, and got talked into buying something a
little too slick . . . But if you like it, buy it.

(PETER *reaches to* HILLY *and tries on the same jacket in his size. It looks different on him, better.*)

JEFF: What are you talking about, it looks great.

PETER: On me.

HILLY: It really does.

PETER: Hilly, the damage.

HILLY: Nine twenty-five.

PETER: It's a deal.

(PETER *and* JEFF *are with* HILLY *at the cash register.* JEFF *asks quietly.*)

JEFF: Hilly, do you have a boyfriend?

HILLY: I have a fiancé.

JEFF: Isn't that romantic? Do me a service, answer this question. How are your morals?

PETER: Dad . . .

HILLY (*defiantly*): I'm working on them.

(PETER *has his eye on* CAROL *across the room.*)

JEFF: Good answer. (*He sees his son watching* CAROL.) Isn't Carol beautiful?

PETER: Yeah, in a quick-trip-to-Acapulco kind of way.

JEFF: Acapulco? . . . Palm Springs.

(*At the counter, they wait for the cashier to complete the credit card business. The card is denied.*)

CASHIER (*whispers*): Peter, can I speak to you for a minute? Your card's been turned down.

JEFF: A collect call from reality.

PETER: You know what I say to reality? I say . . . reverse the charges.

(*Cut to:*)

TITLE SEQUENCE 4

Cut to:

INTERIOR: KEVIN BULASKY'S OFFICE. DAY.

KEVIN BULASKY *sits in an agency conference room.* PETER *stands at the end of a long table, with five other agents. The beginning of this is*

strained: everyone knows what is coming, and nobody wants to be
direct. The scene is quick, tense.

> KEVIN: No, Peter, this hasn't been a good year for the
> agency!
>
> PETER: Things'll get better.
>
> KEVIN: We hope so.
>
> PETER: The economy.
>
> KEVIN: Yeah.
>
> PETER: We just have to hang in there.
>
> KEVIN: A lot of companies are dying.

(KEVIN *crosses the room.*)

> PETER: Well, they don't have the imagination. Entertain-
> ment is recession proof. The revenues are holding
> steady.
>
> KEVIN: Costs keep going up.
>
> PETER (*knows what's coming*): Kevin, I do a lot of busi-
> ness for this company.
>
> KEVIN: No, Peter, you don't. You're bringing in just about
> what we pay you, a little less than three hundred thou-
> sand dollars a year. You are down to six writers, and they
> are hacks, frankly. They haven't grown because you
> don't push them, and you don't push them because you
> don't push yourself. Clients come to you, or came to you,
> because they wanted to be around you. You're a guy
> who people want to be around. But you don't know how
> to close a deal anymore. You don't take the details of the
> business seriously anymore. And you follow your dick a
> little too much.

(KEVIN *pauses.* PETER *thinks. Everyone watches him for his reaction.*)

> PETER (*simply*): I quit.
>
> KEVIN: We're not asking you to quit.
>
> PETER: Well, why should I stay if you're going to insult
> me?
>
> KEVIN: It isn't an insult. It's an intervention. It's . . . part of
> your education. We're trying to help you. You can turn
> yourself around.
>
> PETER: No. I quit. This is actually good news, you know.

I mean, I'm never going to be the head of this company, am I, Kevin?

KEVIN: Probably not.

PETER: Then why in the hell should I stay here? You tell me! (*Getting a little weird for the others in the room.*) You know what, I've been just a little too co-dependent here, taking care of other people's feelings instead of my own, and I think that's been my problem. I have not visualized clearly enough, what I really want. And that's going to change. You think I'm mad at you, I'm not mad at you. This is actually kind of a gift, you know, I welcome this. I, I welcome what my next step in my journey is going to be. And so I quit. Good-bye, Kevin, good-bye, guys.

(PETER *leaves. His eyes are wet.*

Cut to:)

INTERIOR: BEDROOM. LATE AFTERNOON.

PETER (*offscreen*): Do this for me. Please, come for me, just come, that's it, you're so sweet, you're so sweet . . .

(*Now we see her. She rises into the frame.*)

ALISON (*as she comes*): No, no, no.

PETER: Are you happy now?

(*She's younger than he is. He watches her.*)

ALISON: You took a brave leap today, Peter. And you did the right thing; they're not a very good agency. You're just scared, and it's normal to feel scared.

PETER: I'm not scared. Do I look scared?

ALISON: Don't ask me to go by how you look, hmmm, you always look great, that's one of the scary things about you, nobody knows what you're thinking.

PETER: I'm thinking about you, Alison.

(*He looks up at her sweetly, and he kisses her as he leaves. She waves good-bye.*)

* * *

INTERIOR: PETER AND KATHERINE'S HOUSE. DAY.

Close-up. An old Western is on TV, black and white. PETER *is in his entertainment room, watching projection TV, with a full surround sound system. The house is in Beverly Hills, the absolute triumph of the most interesting taste of the last ten years.*

The art on the walls is the best of the 80s, also more obscure early twentieth-century California art.

Someone comes into the room. He looks up. Katherine carries a shopping bag. For a moment, she stands in the way of the television. Then she comes to him, gives him a kiss. He freezes the video.

PETER: It's interesting, isn't it?

(As he talks, she hovers close to him. He feels guilty and doesn't want her that close, but she persists. She kisses him on the cheek, but something keeps her there. Then, surprising him, she kisses him on the mouth. He doesn't want to give her this right now, but she forces it.)

KATHERINE: What?

PETER *(over his anxiety, trying to make this light, but also to get away)*: Laser discs are better than video tape, it's obvious, but vinyl, you know, real records, sound better than CDs. Digital is weird. What are you doing? What are you doing?

(She takes a deep breath through her nose, smelling him, and then she closes her eyes, and we are back in the dark with her, listening to PETER. *He changes the subject, but we know that he knows that she knows.)*

KATHERINE: Where have you been?

PETER: The gym.

KATHERINE: Mmm-hmmm. You must have had quite a workout.

PETER: I did, I was . . . I have a lot of tension.

KATHERINE: You needed to sweat.

PETER: Yes.

KATHERINE: You're still sweating.

PETER: Well, what can I say, I've got a lot on my mind.

KATHERINE: You can tell me what's bothering you, Peter, I'm your wife.

(The phone rings. He answers, saved by the bell.)

PETER: Hello?

(*A voice on the phone, annoyingly friendly, a* SALESMAN.)

SALESMAN: Peter Witner?

PETER: Yeah?

SALESMAN: Congratulations, Peter, you've been selected as a grand prize winner in a nationwide competition. And you're eligible now for one of three fantastic grand prizes!

PETER: Are you proud of yourself? Is this what you wanted to be when you grew up? (*He hangs up.*) God-damn telephone salesmen! Who are these people?

(KATHERINE *watches him. She sees that he is relieved for this distraction.*)

KATHERINE: You were saying . . .

PETER (*okay, you want to hear the truth?*): I quit work today.

KATHERINE: You quit work?

PETER: Yeah.

KATHERINE: You quit without telling me you were going to quit?

PETER: I'm telling you now.

(*He walks across the room toward the kitchen. She chases him.*)

KATHERINE (*bewildered*): Peter!

PETER: What!

KATHERINE: This was a bad time for you to quit. I lost my biggest account today. Everybody's cutting back. You know, there really is no work anymore. Would you listen to me! By the time I pay for materials and staff, I'm not even breaking even. And now you go and quit. What are you going to do?

PETER: The question is what are we going to do. That's the question, what are we going to do. We're a couple.

KATHERINE: You're not behaving like someone in a couple, Peter. You didn't have to quit.

(*She walks away and grabs her shopping bag. He follows her to the bedroom upstairs.*)

PETER: What'd you buy?

KATHERINE: Nothing.

PETER: Expensive nothing. Your business is crashing, and you go shopping?

KATHERINE: You'd do the same. And they were on sale.

PETER: Don't apologize.

(*He comes up behind her and grabs her by the waist.*)

KATHERINE: No!

PETER: Come on. I want to see what you bought.

KATHERINE: I don't like any of it. It's all going back.

(*He kisses her neck. He finds the strap to Sarah's talisman.*)

PETER: What's this?

KATHERINE (*covering*): Oh . . . it's just some, you know, hippie thing Sarah gave me.

(*He turns the lights down.*)

KATHERINE: What is this?

PETER: You need a massage.

KATHERINE: Fine, I'll call Luisa.

PETER: No, from me, now.

KATHERINE: You're going to try to fuck me, I don't want to fuck you right now.

PETER: I'm not going to do anything you don't want to do.

(*She walks out of the frame.*

Cut to:)

INTERIOR: BEDROOM. DAY.

A few minutes later, KATHERINE *is on the bed, face down.* PETER *has massage oil, and he is rubbing her back. He moves to her shoulders. She grunts with pleasure.*

PETER: This is nice, isn't it?

KATHERINE: Hmm.

PETER: Yes, this is very nice.

KATHERINE: Hmm.

PETER: It's a strange place to have a massage like this, though, isn't it? (*His voice changes; it is becoming thicker, sexier.*) In a restaurant. With people watching.

(KATHERINE *groans a little. He is teasing her now; it has gone from massage to sex. And this fantasy is her weak spot. He knows it.*)

KATHERINE: You're not playing fair.

PETER: All those people at the bar are watching us.

KATHERINE (*giving in*): What does the bartender look like?

PETER (*killing her with this*): Like an old truck. Like a beautiful, old truck. Uh-oh, here he comes, he's walking around the bar, and he's coming this way . . . and I think he wants to kiss you while I massage your back.

(*He kisses her.*)

PETER: Close your eyes, keep your eyes closed. The bartender, the bartender can't control himself. He has to . . . probe a little deeper, a little deeper. There are things he just has to know.

KATHERINE: Like what?

PETER: Like . . . like . . . like this.

(*He's done a brilliant job. She's in his power now. And as he makes love to her, we see that she can give herself to something and that he is still objective; she can come, letting go, but there is something that he holds back.*

Dissolve to:)

INTERIOR: BEDROOM. DAY.

When they finish, she speaks:

KATHERINE: It's not fair, you know. The way you make love to me, it's not fair. It's not real. I don't think you're really here.

PETER: But you like it.

KATHERINE: Maybe it's too easy to like.

(*He moves away from her.*)

PETER: Maybe I shouldn't have quit.

KATHERINE: Maybe not.

PETER: We're not in good shape now, are we, you and I?

KATHERINE: Terrible. There's a lot of things between us that we're not saying.

PETER: Do you love me?

KATHERINE: Do you love me?

PETER: Well, if things get really bad, we'll just throw a big party and blow our brains out.

KATHERINE: And make the guests do the clean up? Please,
that's so . . . unfair to them.

PETER: Well, then, let's throw a party.

KATHERINE: Yeah, that's a lovely idea.

PETER: We haven't done one in six months. I mean, I think
we need it. We need to shake something up, don't you
think? (*A pause.*) Katherine? What do you think? Kather-
ine? Katherine—

(*Cut to:*)

INTERIOR: PETER AND KATHERINE'S HOUSE. FOYER. NIGHT.

KATHERINE *opens the door. She shifts tone again, abruptly, to greet*
JEFF, *this time with* EMILY. *There is a noisy display of kisses and hugs
and compliments.* JEFF *is a little startled by Katherine's dress.*

PETER: Dad!

JEFF: Oh, I hate that word, not in front of Emily, please.

EMILY: I'm Emily.

PETER: Hi, Emily. I'm Peter, this is Katherine. Welcome to
our house.

EMILY: It's a beautiful home. Didn't I see this in *Architec-
tural Digest?*

PETER: *H.G.,* November '89.

JEFF (*to* KATHERINE): You look *great.*

(*The old fox, he'd fuck his daughter-in-law.*)

KATHERINE: Jeff, how was, how was Chicago?

INTERIOR: HOUSE. LIVING ROOM. NIGHT.

*In the corner of the living room is a grand piano with a computer
console attached below the keyboard.*

PETER: Where'd you meet her?

JEFF: Isn't she beautiful?

(PETER *sits at the piano and plays a few bars of Bach, and it sounds
as if he were a real musician.* JEFF *stops him.*)

JEFF: Doesn't the world already know that's the only piece
you play?

PETER: What about this?

(PETER *pushes a button. His recorded tinkling is played back by this modern player piano.*
They walk out toward the pool.)

INTERIOR: HOUSE. DOORWAY. NIGHT.
More people come in, including SUE *with a few friends, one of whom is* MISHA, *good-looking but not aggressively hunky, no leather.*

SUE: Hi.

KATHERINE: Sue. Hi.

SUE: Thanks for inviting me.

KATHERINE: Oh, pleasure.

SUE: This is my friend Misha. This is Katherine.

MISHA: Hi. (*He looks at the plant by the door.*) Very healthy plant.

KATHERINE: Yeah, it is, isn't it.

(*There's a look between them.*)

MISHA: Good nitrogen level.

KATHERINE: Yeah.

(ANNA *arrives.*)

ANNA: Katherine. Hi.

KATHERINE: Anna!

ANNA: Dick sends his regrets.

KATHERINE: Such a shame.

ANNA: How are you?

KATHERINE: I'm fine.

ANNA: Are you really?

KATHERINE: Now stop that.

(*They walk into the party.*)

INTERIOR: HOUSE. TV ROOM. NIGHT.

PETER: Dad, Katherine and I are . . .

JEFF: What?

PETER: Having problems.

JEFF: Two choices.

PETER: Yeah?

JEFF: Ride it out or leave her.

(JEFF *pats* PETER *on the back and leaves.*
Cut to:)

EXTERIOR: HOUSE. OUTSIDE TV ROOM AND LIVING ROOM. NIGHT.
In the living room, we see ELLEN SALTONSTALL *come in the door with*
SARAH FRIEDBERG, *followed by* JEAN LEVY, *fifty, French. A few spiritual*
camp followers are with them.
PETER *brightens when he sees* ELLEN. *She's attractive, thirties, open.*
She's ahead of the group. PETER *is now eating something.*

ELLEN: Peter!

PETER: Ellen!

ELLEN: I have to talk to you.

PETER: Ellen, I have to play host.

ELLEN: It's important.

PETER: Okay.

ELLEN: But we'll talk later.

PETER: Right. Hi, Sarah.

INTERIOR: HOUSE. LIVING ROOM. NIGHT.
And then the introductions. KATHERINE *comes over, too, to give* SARAH
a hug. Things happen all at once. PETER *shakes hands with* JEAN, *who*
never takes his eyes from the eyes of the person he is talking to.

SARAH: How are you, Peter?

ELLEN: We brought a friend. This is Jean Levy. Jean's from
France.

JEAN: Belgium.

SARAH: La Belgique, he's a teacher. A spiritual teacher.

(*And then in the dining room, he sees* KATHERINE *talking to* ALISON
and her date, RYAN. *We see* RYAN *introduce her to* ALISON. ALISON
smiles at PETER *as though there is nothing between them, but* KATHER-
INE *picks up something. We see* JEAN *in the background, watching*
before he goes outside.)

KATHERINE: Peter, do you remember Ryan?

PETER: Yeah, sure.

KATHERINE: He used to do brochures with me, but now he's a production designer. And this is . . . Alison?

ALISON: Alison Gale, yeah.

PETER: Hi.

ALISON: Hi.

KATHERINE: You must know her, she's an agent.

PETER: No.

ALISON (*simultaneous*): Yes.

PETER (*recovers*): Yeah . . . William Morris, right?

ALISON: Right, right— (*To* RYAN:) Drink time.

(*And she pulls him away.* PETER *and* KATHERINE *face each other for a moment and then turn away from each other.*)

PETER: Excuse me.

(*She knows.*

Time cut:)

EXTERIOR: THE PARTY. POOL AREA. LATER.

Two women walk together. BETTINA *is talking.*

BETTINA (*to* NANCY): Did you see the painting on the second floor? The one with the three ships? God, I love that painting.

(PETER *studies them from a buffet.* NANCY *walks away.*)

PETER: Ed Ruscha. The first painting I ever bought.

BETTINA: Bettina. Nice party.

PETER: Peter, glad you think so.

BETTINA: The people are, um, very friendly.

PETER: Can I ask you a question?

BETTINA: You can ask me any question.

PETER: Really?

BETTINA: Really.

PETER: Any question?

BETTINA: Sure.

PETER: How are your morals tonight?

BETTINA: What does that mean?

PETER: How are your morals? Knowing the difference between good and evil, do you care?

BETTINA: That's a strange thing to say when your wife is standing twenty feet away.

PETER: Mm-hmm. Who'd you come here with?

BETTINA: My friend Nancy.

PETER: So, uh . . . (*one second of awkwardness*) how are your morals?

(*A pause. In the background, we see* KATHERINE *talking to someone, but she is distracted by* PETER *and* BETTINA. *And then she sees* MISHA *watching her watch her husband flirt with another woman.*)

BETTINA: Sort of . . . weak. And yours?

PETER: You know, I don't know, I just can't seem to find them.

BETTINA: Don't look too hard, you might spoil all the fun.

(*Her look: Did you expect this? Can you go all the way? And she walks away.*
Cut to:)

EXTERIOR: PATIO ENTRANCE. LATER.

JEAN *approaches.*

JEAN (*to* PETER, *out of a mystical nowhere*): Nobody taught you to be a man.

PETER (*stunned*): What did you say?

(*The sound and the lighting change.* JEAN *and* PETER *are momentarily alone in a metaphysical bubble.* PETER *is in his thrall; he can't resist him; and* JEAN *looks into Peter's soul, making* PETER *anxious, uncomfortable.*)

JEAN: It bothers you to be looked at this way.

PETER: Well, it's not what I'm used to.

JEAN: You need it. You're in trouble.

PETER: Everybody's in trouble.

JEAN: I see blocked energies, energies turned back on themselves. I see you trying to cancel yourself out.

PETER: What about her? What about that woman over there.

(*He points to* KATHERINE, *who is talking to* SARAH.)

JEAN: Your wife . . . shares some of your weakness. Also, she's angry at you. She doesn't trust you. We have a retreat center in Lone Pine. Come to Lone Pine. You need it. Both of you. Don't be afraid of change.

PETER: But I am afraid of change. Every time I make a change, I regret it.

(PETER *breaks away from* JEAN. *The light and sound return to normal.* Cut to:)

EXTERIOR: BY THE POOL. NIGHT.

PETER *is stopped by* ALISON, *who has been looking for him.*

ALISON: Peter, Ryan invited me and I didn't make the connection, because your wife invited him, and I mean, he said Katherine, but he didn't say the last name, and even then, I don't think I would have made the connection myself.

PETER: Don't sweat it.

ALISON: Okay. Thank you. I mean, I'm not the biggest believer in monogamy either, you know that, but this is a little embarrassing for me.

PETER: Hmm-mm. So is Ryan the love of your life?

ALISON: How dare you be jealous? God . . . No.

(*Cut to:*)

INTERIOR: LIVING ROOM. LATER.

LAURA *and* LYLE *come into the party. Both are terribly thin.* LAURA *walks with a cane.*

She is wearing makeup to cover her sarcomas. Her husband is LYLE. *With them is* MARY NETTER, *sort of an Ojai Wasp, New Age in style (shawl, drop earrings), in her sixties. As we leave them, we will see her greet* JEAN *and* SARAH; *they all know each other.*

PETER: Mary, hi. Laura, hi, Lyle, I thought you were all outside. How are you, Laura?

LAURA (*smiling weakly*): Never better.

PETER: Well, what can I get you? What do you need? Do you want to sit down? Do you want something? What can I do?

LYLE: We just came to look at people tonight.

PETER: Okay, you look all you want. Here she is, here she is.

(KATHERINE *comes over and kisses* LAURA *and* LYLE.)

KATHERINE: Laura, God, how are you . . . How are you feeling?

LAURA: Good.

KATHERINE: Do you want to sit down?

LAURA: No, no, I want to stand.

KATHERINE: Lyle, God. Ohh.

(PETER *sees* ELLEN. *She beckons to him.*)

PETER: Excuse me.

EXTERIOR: PETER AND KATHERINE'S HOUSE. NIGHT.

ELLEN *turns to him and walks backward. She is teasing him as he bumps into* PAUL HARTMANN *and his friend* CHRIS. *They are gay, and* PAUL *carries a basket with a sleeping baby in it.*

PAUL: Hey, Peter!

PETER: Paul, how are you? Hi, Chris.

PAUL: We couldn't get a baby-sitter tonight.

PETER: Oh, isn't she cute?

PAUL: I didn't want a baby-sitter tonight. I need this as much as she does.

PETER: Excuse me.

(PETER *sees* ELLEN. PAUL *sees that* PETER *is distracted.*)

PAUL: I talked to Kevin this morning.

PETER: Really?

PAUL: He's being very good about all this, and as far as the world thinks, you left over a compensation issue. He's talked to a few studio people for you. He likes you, you know.

PETER: I don't give a shit if he likes me, Paul, I quit. It was my idea.

PAUL: Would you be interested in heading up business affairs for a television syndicator?

PETER: Well, that's not exactly what I had in mind.

PAUL: Fine, Peter, just tell me what you want. I may not be able to get it, but I can't even try unless you know. What exactly do you want now? How do you want to make a living? Do you want to work for a studio? Do you want to work for an agency? Do you wanna go into business with a producer?

PETER: I wanna do something, Paul, I wanna, you know, just, I want to do something, you know, that—that uses the best of me, Paul, okay. That uses the best of me.

PAUL: Well, that's a beginning.

PETER: Yeah. So what would you say if I told you I was thinking about getting out of Hollywood?

PAUL: Peter, when you sail beyond the horizon, you fall off the edge of the world. Forget what they taught you in school. The earth is flat. Look, we really can't stay. I haven't seen Susanna all week. We're taking her to Santa Barbara tomorrow. You're not listening to me!

PETER: Good night, Paul.

(PETER *nods and follows* ELLEN. *He catches up to her.*)

ELLEN: Cados, Cados, Cados, Adonay, Eloy, Zena, Oth, Ochimanuel, Wisdom, Way, Life, Virtue . . .

EXTERIOR: BETWEEN THE HOUSE AND THE POOL SHED AT THE BAR. NIGHT.

On KATHERINE: *she is watching* PETER *and* ELLEN. MISHA *comes up behind her.*

MISHA: He cheats on you.

KATHERINE: How do you know?

MISHA: The way he talks to women, his body language. When he goes on business trips, he takes off his wedding ring.

KATHERINE: How do you know this?

MISHA: You don't deserve that. You're a trophy.

KATHERINE: There's a lot of dust on this old trophy.

MISHA: You just need to be polished.

(KATHERINE *laughs to herself; this is getting sexy. She looks at him. She sees him; she sees the possibilities.*)

KATHERINE: You're not so young.

MISHA: I'm not sixteen.

KATHERINE: I bet you've been around the block, Mister Smarty.

MISHA: A couple of times.

KATHERINE: More than a couple.

MISHA: So I've run a marathon or two.

KATHERINE (*laughs, it is sex now*): I bet you have.

MISHA: Do something stupid. Leave the party with me.

KATHERINE: I'm not going to leave my own party with a twenty-six-year-old . . . actor?

MISHA: I'm not an actor.

KATHERINE (*a cute double take*): Well, what?

MISHA: I'm a businessman. I own a coffee house. It's called Insomnia.

KATHERINE: Oh, I've been there.

MISHA (*this is about sex*): I've seen you there. And you've seen me there.

KATHERINE: Yes.

MISHA: You've been watching me all night.

KATHERINE: Yes.

MISHA: And we've been watching each other. (*A pause. They are committing themselves to something.*) I won't bite.

KATHERINE: Then you're like all the men in this town, all talk, no teeth.

(*He smiles and starts to leave. She follows, unnoticed by everyone except* SARAH, JEAN, *and* ANNA.)

SARAH (*to* JEAN): Experience and sensation.

(ANNA *stops* KATHERINE.)

ANNA: Conscience police!

KATHERINE: You have no jurisdiction in this territory.

ANNA: What are you doing?

KATHERINE: I'm following my bliss.

(*And she takes Misha's hand.*)

* * *

EXTERIOR: HOUSE. NIGHT.

Back to PETER: *he is alone now.* JEAN *approaches.*

>JEAN: She left.
>
>PETER: Who?
>
>JEAN: Your wife. She left with someone. (*Off of Peter's stunned, embarrassed silence.*) You must embrace the thing that hurts you.
>
>PETER: What does that mean?
>
>JEAN: Live with the question.

(*Dissolve to:*)

INTERIOR: INSOMNIA. NIGHT.

KATHERINE *and* MISHA *are making love.* MISHA *groans. A little of Katherine's face. She's having fun, but there's more to it than that: this is what she needs.*

>KATHERINE: I've never done this before. My husband does it.
>
>MISHA: I like you.
>
>KATHERINE: It's funny how people connect, isn't it?

INTERIOR: LIVING ROOM. NIGHT.

PETER *sits on the sofa facing the piano.* PETER *is alone, watching the piano play itself, playing Debussy.*

EXTERIOR: PATIO. MORNING.

On PETER, *isolated, and we hear Katherine's angry voice:*

>KATHERINE: Is it my fault things are so fucked up between us? Are you going to tell me that it's my fault?

(*Now we see* KATHERINE. PETER *is eating chicken out of a Ziploc bag.*)

>PETER: I didn't say it was your fault. It's not a right or wrong thing.
>
>KATHERINE: Oh, please, could you just tell the truth? I mean, could you tell the truth for once in your life?
>
>PETER: You wouldn't recognize it.

KATHERINE: Okay, okay, so—how have I held you back?

PETER: I didn't say you held me back. One person cannot hold another person back. That's a judgement. There's no victim here. I said I feel held back, Katherine. These are my feelings. Like what you did, last night, okay, you know that hurts me. I feel hurt by that. See, but, okay, maybe that's a gift, maybe that's my wake-up call. I realize my life isn't on track. I mean, maybe I'm on a detour, I'm on a subpath, so I need support, you know I don't feel any support from you. Like quitting my job, you know that's a subpath. But do I hear, great, honey, great, I'm with you, I hope you find your dream. I hear, WHAT ARE WE GOING TO DO FOR MONEY. I mean, what is money. Money is not money. Money is just an expression of something else. Money will express itself. If we need money, money will express itself. It's like love. If there's love here, love will express itself. I mean, these are my feelings. Support—I just need support, Katherine! You know I need a push! I need a goddamn push!

KATHERINE: You'd fall over. You'd break.

PETER: Yeah, you'd like to think so, wouldn't you? I mean, I'm trying to get to something here . . . get to the bottom of something here, and the least you could do is try to be nice. I mean, it's your big weapon, isn't it? It's your . . . your . . . it's what everyone adores about you—how nice you are.

KATHERINE: I wasn't nice last night.

PETER (*a sudden and unexpected shift: now he is cute, and she has got him*): No . . . You were bad.

KATHERINE: Don't be cute! You quit your job, with no place else to go. You can't afford to be cute.

PETER: It's just my inner child showing through.

KATHERINE: Your inner child is running us into bankruptcy. Why don't you get in touch with your inner adult?

(*And she storms away. He throws the food down.*)

* * *

EXTERIOR: PATIO. DAY. LATER.

PETER *sits, contemplating. The mood has changed; the confrontation is over. After a moment:*

KATHERINE: Why are we so awful?

PETER: You're the mystic in this family, aren't we supposed to think positively?

KATHERINE: I'm trying, like I'm trying to find work. But I've called everybody. Nobody needs a graphic designer. We have to find some work, Peter. We have about thirty days left in the bank, and then we are broke. And if we don't find some money, we're going to have to start selling paintings, one by one, and then the house.

PETER: Yeah okay. Cut to the chase.

KATHERINE: I hate that line.

PETER: Look, are you going to criticize everything I say, or are you going to talk to me?

KATHERINE: Should we get a divorce?

PETER: What? Who's talking about a divorce, Katherine?

KATHERINE: I don't know.

PETER: What, you sleep with a guy one night, and you want a divorce?

KATHERINE: No. I don't know.

PETER: Well, what? Are you in love with him?

KATHERINE: No.

PETER: Well, what?

KATHERINE: Well, I need some space, space. We both need space. I'm so in love with you, Peter, but I'm going out of my mind. If I had some money, I'd buy a condo, you know, but I can't even afford rent. And I can't kick you out of the house. It's yours as much as it's mine. We've got to get some money, Peter.

PETER: Well, I'm trying, baby, I'm trying.

KATHERINE: Yeah, well, we have to try harder. Peter, this is what I've been thinking. We both stay living in the house, but we have our own lives. You know, we live separately. Just for awhile. Okay? I could take my office; you could take the bedroom. Just for a while. What do you think?

(PETER *nods*.)
>PETER: You take the bedroom.
>KATHERINE: Very generous. That was very generous. But it was my idea. You take the bedroom.
>PETER: Okay.
>KATHERINE: Okay.

EXTERIOR: HOUSE. NIGHT.
KATHERINE *and* MISHA *are leaving on a date.* PETER *watches from a window.*

EXTERIOR: PATIO/SITTING AREA. NEXT MORNING.
JEAN *moderates a group with* PETER *and* KATHERINE. ELLEN *is also there as Jean's assistant.*
>JEAN: What are you afraid of?
>PETER: Poverty.
>KATHERINE: Work.
>PETER: We're not afraid of work. You work, I work.
>KATHERINE: No, no, I mean real work. That's what we're afraid of. Jobs, regular jobs, by the hour, no expense account.
>PETER: No expense account? Yikes! God, I'd kill myself.
>JEAN: Really?
>ELLEN: What Jean means is that everyone is good at something, but sometimes they don't want to admit what that is, because they think that it might be something that they shouldn't do. So what are you good at?
>JEAN: If the two of you could do anything right now, go anywhere, where would you go, what would you do?
>KATHERINE: Shopping. Oh, my God! What did I just say?
>PETER (*laughing*): What!
>KATHERINE (*amazed*): We'd go shopping.
>PETER (*still laughing*): That's right. That's what we're good at. Shopping and talking.
>JEAN: There's your answer. You know, in Chinese the word for *crisis* is the same as the word for *opportunity*.

PETER: Now, if I ask him to explain that, is he going to tell me to live with the question?

KATHERINE: No, no, I know what he means. It's so—it's so clear, it's brilliant. He wants us to open a store. Isn't that right? Shopping and talking? A store.

PETER: What kind of store? What are we selling?

JEAN: *Live* with the question.

(*Cut to:*)

EXTERIOR: STREETS OF LOS ANGELES. DAY.

KATHERINE *and* PETER *are driving in Katherine's Scout. They are looking at stores and the* FOR RENT, FOR SALE, *and* FOR LEASE *signs that populate the street.*

PETER: Yeah, an eyeglass store!

KATHERINE: No, what do you mean, an eyeglass store?

PETER: Glasses!

KATHERINE: You need a special license for that.

PETER: Yeah, well—

KATHERINE: Technically, anyway. I know, I know, what about a franchise for a copy store, we could open a Kinko's or a Pip—

PETER: Oh, God.

KATHERINE: Well, what's wrong with that?

PETER: Oh, God.

KATHERINE: Oh, God, what do you mean, oh, God?

PETER (*simultaneously*): Oh, God. I mean, Xerox machines, five cents a page, endless streams of displaced midlevel insurance executives coming by with a resume. Man alive—

KATHERINE: There's a lot, there's a lot of—those—midlevel—insurance—executives needing these resumes copied. You know, five cents a page adds up.

PETER: To what? Money? So what, there are a lot of ways to make money. They don't have to be so goddamn boring. I mean, look, I know I'm sick, I know I got problems, I know I worry about looking cool. But you

worry about looking cool too; now don't tell me you
don't.

KATHERINE: I know. But I'm working on it.

(*Cut to:*)

INTERIOR: KATHERINE'S OFFICE/BEDROOM. NIGHT.

MISHA, *in a towel, looks at some of Katherine's designs on her draft-
ing table.* KATHERINE *is disrobing. We hear a car pulling into the
driveway. Stay with the couple for a moment.*
Cut to:

EXTERIOR: HOUSE. NIGHT.

PETER *and* ALISON *get out of Peter's BMW and walk into the house
under Katherine's window.*
Cut to:

INTERIOR: KATHERINE'S OFFICE/BEDROOM. LATER.

MISHA *and* KATHERINE *are making love.*
Match cut to:

INTERIOR: LIVING ROOM. NIGHT.

A painting of a kissing couple. We glide through the room to find
ALISON *playing the piano. She plays something, and it is beautiful,
Chopin.*

INTERIOR: KATHERINE'S ROOM. NIGHT.

KATHERINE *can hear the music. She has to stop.*

INTERIOR: LIVING ROOM. NIGHT.

The mood changes. PETER *comes over to the piano, and he kisses her,
and she misses a note, and then he puts his hands on her. She stops.*

She turns around and puts her elbows on the keyboard, producing a wild chord. He kisses her, and they begin to make love against the keyboard.
Cut to:

INTERIOR: KATHERINE'S ROOM. NIGHT.
KATHERINE *has to stop making love.*

INTERIOR: KATHERINE'S BEDROOM. NIGHT.
It is too dark to really see anything. Then Peter's voice:
PETER: Hipocracy!
KATHERINE: What?
(*The door opens a little.* PETER *barges in.* KATHERINE, *in bed, is still mostly in the dark.*)
PETER: The hip aristocracy, the hipocracy, get it?
KATHERINE: No.
PETER: Hello. The name of the store, Katherine. Hipocracy. And what are we selling, baby? We're selling clothes. That's what we're selling. We're selling clothes. That's what we're going to call it. We'll call it Hipocracy. And we're going to be rich! We're going to have the first small department store for all of the hipocrites. I mean, if we're so good at shopping, we'll do the shopping for the customers, and the store carries the stock of our best taste, a few great shirts, a few great dresses.
KATHERINE: But, well, how is it going to be different from any other store?
PETER: I knew you'd ask that. I knew you'd ask that question. The stock changes all the time, so the customers keep coming back to see what we have from week to week. It'll be the store people go to when they don't have the time, but they come to us when they know what they're looking for.
KATHERINE: Yeah, what they need.
PETER: Perfect, listen to the slogan: Hipocracy, It's Not What You're Looking For, dash dash, It's What You Need.

(*She thinks it can work. She is beaming. The shock of a good idea.
The sheets pull back from behind* KATHERINE. *It is* MISHA.)

MISHA: It does have possibilities.

EXTERIOR: STOREFRONT. DAY.

KATHERINE *and* PETER *drive up, go inside, and greet a realtor, who
waves a hand over the large space.*

INTERIOR: AUCTION HOUSE. DAY.

*Two of their paintings are on the stand. The auctioneer's gavel comes
down.*

AUCTIONEER: Sold!

INTERIOR: HIPOCRACY. DAY.

It is raw space. We are in the middle of a ceremony. ELLEN *runs and*
JEAN *walks around the space silently, feeling the vibrations, while*
PETER *and* KATHERINE *watch.*

ELLEN: We need a mirror, behind the cash register. Here.
The reflection will double your wealth, Peter.

PETER: Really.

JEAN: And the dressing rooms, where do you want to put
them?

KATHERINE: The dressing rooms are right . . . here.

JEAN: No.

ELLEN: Not in a direct line with the door.

KATHERINE: Oh.

ELLEN: All the energy from the street . . . no one will feel
comfortable.

KATHERINE: Right.

JEAN: Peter, did you bring these objects that are valuable
to you?

KATHERINE/PETER: Yeah.

(PETER *and* KATHERINE *bring out a few small things: objects from
their house, something precious to each. And so a little shrine is
arranged.*)

PETER: It's going to work. I feel it.

JEAN: If it's meant to succeed . . . But the experience will be good for you.

(*Close on a finely drawn rendering of the completed store.* KATHERINE *makes a mark where it should go.*

Match cut to:)

INTERIOR: HIPOCRACY. OPENING NIGHT PARTY.

The drawing drops away, and we are in the completed *store.*

PETER *is dressed in a beautiful suit.*

The store is filled with friends for the opening party.

JEFF *and* EMILY, *then the women, men from neighboring stores. Also* ELLEN, JEAN, *and* LYLE.

SUE, *Katherine's former assistant, helps out, but* KATHERINE *has had the party catered, of course, and the display is generous.*

PETER: Dad—

JEFF: Working for a living. What's it like?

PETER: I feel clean, Dad. I feel clean.

JEFF: I think you're very brave to open an expensive clothing store on the same street where all the other stores sell antiques and toilets.

PETER: Come on, Dad, this is a new beginning for Katherine and me, give us your blessing.

JEFF: Well, I wish you the best of luck, really.

PETER: Thank you. Dad.

(ELLEN *and* JEAN *walk nearby.*)

ELLEN: The mirrors behind the cash register. They are too small. Do you think that will make a difference?

JEAN: It might.

(*On* KATHERINE. KATHERINE *and* ANNA. KATHERINE *is showing* ANNA *the belts.*)

ANNA: Now, that's lovely.

KATHERINE: The belt? Isn't it fabulous?

ANNA: Hmmm.

KATHERINE: The leather is Italian, and the buckle comes from a designer in New York.

ANNA (*we are not convinced by her*): Oh, God, it's gorgeous.

KATHERINE: We think so.

ANNA: Yeah. How much is it?

(ANNA *looks at the tag, which is hard to read.*)

KATHERINE: Four hundred.

ANNA: It's four hundred bucks?

KATHERINE: You know what, it would look wonderful with—you know, that blue jacket of yours with the zip. (*You know the one . . .*)

ANNA: Right. You were there when I bought that.

KATHERINE: Oh, I was too.

ANNA: Right. So—(*a moment between them,* ANNA *knows what is expected of her*) well, great.

KATHERINE: Oh, great!

ANNA: Yeah!

KATHERINE: Great, well, I'll wrap it—

ANNA: Okay. (*She starts to write the check.*) Okay, so do I make this out to you or the store? Hypocrisy?

KATHERINE (*sees the check*): A-C-Y, not I-C-Y.

ANNA: Oh.

KATHERINE: Yeah. (*She forgot the tax.*) You know what? Actually, it's four hundred thirty-three. The tax—

(ANNA *tears up the check.*)

ANNA: Oh, right. The tax. Okay. So, it's just, it's a really classic belt. It's wonderful. Okay . . . (*spells it right this time*) A-C-Y.

KATHERINE: Right. Like *aristocracy.*

ANNA: I get it, I get it. That's clever.

KATHERINE: Sue! Would you wrap this, please?

ANNA: You don't wrap?

KATHERINE (*confidentially to* ANNA): I'm terrible at wrapping.

(*On* PETER: *he hears the call to* SUE.)

PETER: Are you making a sale? Yoo-hoo?

KATHERINE: Yeah.

(*She nods. He gives a thumbs up.*)

PETER (*loudly*): Quiet, quiet, everyone. Quiet, please, quiet. First dollar! First dollar.

(*Their friends applaud a little too loudly.*)

EXTERIOR: HIPOCRACY. DAY.

The sign in the window CLOSED *is turned to* OPEN. *The door is unlocked.* PETER *and* KATHERINE *are open for business.*

PETER: First day.

KATHERINE: Yep. This is very weird. Isn't it? I'm not used to this.

PETER: Ahh, you're doing great.

KATHERINE: I am?

PETER: I'm the schmuck, you know. I know I'm a jerk.

KATHERINE: Peter . . .

PETER: It's true. I'm half-cool but not really.

KATHERINE: You have to let go of all that.

PETER: Why did you marry me?

KATHERINE: What?

PETER: Why did you marry me?

KATHERINE: I was in love with you.

PETER: I was in love with you too, but why did you marry me?

KATHERINE: You were smart, you were handsome, you were funny. You were a good lover. We had fun.

(*A* MAN *and a* WOMAN *pass by and stop.*)

PETER (*under his breath, the way he urged* ALISON *in sex*): That's it, that's it, just come, come to me, that's it.

(*They come into the store.*)

PETER (*whispers*): Yes! (*Loud.*) Hello!

KATHERINE: Were you looking for anything special?

WOMAN: No. (*She looks at a dress.*) Eighteen hundred dollars?

(*And she picks at a few sleeves, touches a few T-shirts.*)

MAN: Get a belt.

WOMAN: Let me look.

MAN: Look. (*To* PETER, *man-to-man:*) She wants to look.

PETER: She wants to buy.

(*She looks up sharply at* PETER.)

WOMAN: I want to look. I'll decide for myself when I want to buy. Do I need you to tell me what I want to do?

PETER: Get out, we're closed.

MAN: What?

PETER: We're not really open. This isn't really a store. It's a movie set, we're doing research for a movie. And, uh, this isn't real life. So, uh, you know, I mean, I don't need this. Just, you know, there's nothing here really for sale, so get out!

(KATHERINE, *fuming, storms out the back to the alley.*)

MAN: Let's go.

WOMAN: Is this a TV show?

PETER: No, it's not. Get out. Get out!

WOMAN: This isn't really a store?

PETER: No, and you're not really a customer. So, bye-bye.

(*The* MAN *takes the woman's arm.*)

EXTERIOR: HIPOCRACY ALLEY. DAY.

KATHERINE *paces around, chanting to herself:*

KATHERINE: He-is-insane-this-will-not-work. He-is-insane-this-will-not-work. He-is-insane-this-will-not-work. He-is-insane-this-will-not-work.

(PETER *comes out to the alley, wildly excited and proud.*)

PETER: I made a sale, I made a sale, I made a sale, I'm making a sale, I'm making a sale . . .

(*He lifts her into his arms and goes back in.*
Cut to:)

INTERIOR: HIPOCRACY. DAY.

A man is at the counter.

KATHERINE (*false cheer*): Cash or charge? Peter . . .

PETER: What?

KATHERINE: Will you wrap?

PETER: It's done.

KATHERINE: Thank you very much.

PETER: Your wife will love it.

(*He wraps. The customer leaves.*
Dissolve to:)

INTERIOR: HIPOCRACY. NIGHT.

It is night. KATHERINE *and* PETER *sit at a back table looking over*
receipts.

KATHERINE: Six hundred and fifty dollars.

PETER: Two shirts and a belt, that's not bad. What are you
doing tonight?

KATHERINE: Reading. What about you?

PETER: I don't know. I'm pretty tired.

KATHERINE: You can't come to my room.

PETER: That's not what I was asking.

KATHERINE: Just in case you were thinking of it.

(PETER *stands up, stretches his arms, and spins.*)

INTERIOR: HIPOCRACY. DAY.

A group of rich GERMAN TOURISTS *finish shopping. They love the cloth-*
ing, are talking about it in German to each other. We get the point:
they are buying a ton.

GERMAN TOURIST: Take it all—

(PETER *gives* KATHERINE *the price of each item as she rings each one*
up.)

PETER: One thousand dollars . . .

GERMAN TOURIST: Wow, that's so much cheaper than in
Hamburg. For us shopping here is like for you shopping
in Tijuana.

KATHERINE: My God, we're cheap.

PETER: We're the third world.

(*The* GERMANS *leave.*)

KATHERINE: Seven thousand nine hundred and eighty
dollars.

PETER: What?

KATHERINE: Eight thousand dollars. It's working. It's actually working. We had an idea, we took a risk, and it's working.

PETER: Oh ye, oh ye of little faith.

(*They start to dance around the store, wildly, emotionally. He gives her a hug. She hugs him back. They start to kiss. He pushes her back into a dressing room. They pull the curtain. They start to make love in the dressing room. It is fun; they are laughing at themselves.*)

KATHERINE: Oh, my God.

PETER: You're in a clothing store, you're in the dressing room of a clothing store. There are people outside walking on the sidewalk, window shopping.

KATHERINE: Can anyone see us?

PETER: Would you like that? Would you like that?

(*They're making love now.*)

KATHERINE: I miss you.

(*A customer comes into the store. They try to be quiet.*)

KATHERINE: Oh, my God. A customer.

PETER: What? There'll be another—

KATHERINE: No, no.

PETER: No—wait.

(*She breaks it off. He knows she is right and knows he is weak for not having admitted the necessity.* KATHERINE *comes swinging out of the dressing room as casually and brightly as she can.*)

KATHERINE: Hello, oh, you're a six, right? I have something that I think you're really going to like.

(PETER *comes out, tucking in his shirt. The customer sees this. Cut to:*)

INTERIOR: HIPOCRACY. MONTAGE.

We dissolve through a series of days and nights of business at Hipocracy. KATHERINE *and* PETER *waiting, no customers. The business is failing.*

* * *

INTERIOR: BEDROOMS. NIGHT.

The phone rings. KATHERINE *reaches over* MISHA *to answer it. In Peter's room, he reaches over* ALISON *to do the same.*

> KATHERINE: Hello?
>
> PETER: Katherine?
>
> KATHERINE: Hello, Peter?
>
> LYLE: It's Lyle.
>
> KATHERINE: Lyle.
>
> LYLE: You better come.
>
> PETER: Okay.

(*Cut to:*)

EXTERIOR: LOS ANGELES STREETS. DAY.

KATHERINE *and* PETER *drive to* LAURA *and Lyle's.* PETER *listens to a KCRW pledge drive.* KATHERINE *turns the radio off.*
Cut to:

INTERIOR: LYLE AND LAURA'S HOUSE. DAY.

A few other men and women are there. A video plays. It is LAURA, *at least six months ago, frail but not obviously dying.*

> LAURA (*on the TV*): Okay, I want to make this as simple as possible. I'm not getting better. And I don't want to go out screaming. I want to be surrounded by the people I love, and I want to say good-bye to them. If I get too sick, Lyle knows what to do. Umm, so anyway, if you're here, I guess it means you were special to me. So I'll see you all soon, I promise, so don't be afraid.

(*The video is over.* LYLE *leads everyone into Laura's bedroom.* LAURA *is in bed, and she looks terrible.*
Everyone gathers around her in the room. LYLE *stirs a bowl of yogurt.* PETER *watches this intently, and* KATHERINE *sees his fascination.* MARY, *from the first party, helps* LYLE *prepare.*)

> LYLE: Is it very bitter?
>
> MARY: Yes, but that's okay.
>
> LYLE: I know that's okay.

(MARY *hands* PETER *a small gong.*)

MARY: Peter, may I please ask you to hold this? It's the masculine principle, and the bowl is the feminine principle, and both together they bring forth the sound vibration of wholeness.

(*The sound is beautiful.*

LYLE *spoons the yogurt into Laura's mouth.* LAURA *holds Lyle's wrist as he does this.*)

LYLE: It's time to say good-bye now.

(*Everyone goes back to the living room, leaving* LYLE *alone with* LAURA. LAURA *and Lyle's love for each other is healing everyone in the room.* PETER *and* KATHERINE *move closer to each other, hold hands.*)

INTERIOR: LAURA AND LYLE'S LIVING ROOM. DAY.

MARY *plays her Tibetan bells. The sound is beautiful, filling the room. There is a picture of Lone Pine on the wall.*

MARY: She's going to the other side now.

PETER: Do you really believe that?

KATHERINE: Let's not turn this into a debate about religion.

MARY: But it's not a debate. I think Peter just wants some comfort. That's what rituals are for.

PETER (*not sure if he believes this is right*): Suicide . . .

MARY: Self-deliverance.

PETER: I thought you didn't go to Heaven if you kill yourself.

MARY: The traditions don't agree. I think you can. If you're clear about it. If you're not, you come back. And you've learned something.

PETER: It scares me.

MARY: It takes courage. It takes just as much courage to die as to live.

(PETER *doesn't want to hear this, and he leaves the circle and walks away.* KATHERINE *comes to him after a moment. He grabs her; they hug.*

A change in the sound of the Tibetan bell from the other room. They look up. Freeze frame.)

* * *

INTERIOR: HIPOCRACY. DAY.

KATHERINE *walks inside and looks at herself in a mirror. She is unhappy.* PETER *is at the front of the store.*

PETER: Katherine! . . . Katherine! What do you think?

KATHERINE: Huh?

(*One of the racks has a sign above it now:* SALE 10% OFF.)

PETER: I mean we don't need a sign in the window, do we? Not yet, do we?

KATHERINE: If we're going to do it, we should do it.

PETER: A small sign.

KATHERINE: If they can't see it, what's the difference?

(*They put the sign in the window.*)

KATHERINE: Let's turn off the music.

PETER: Why?

KATHERINE: Just turn it off.

PETER: You can't have a store without music. Everyone has music.

KATHERINE: Everyone is sick.

(*Suddenly,* KATHERINE *sees her friends* ANNA *and* TINA *pass by outside the store. She runs outside.*)

EXTERIOR: HIPOCRACY. DAY.

KATHERINE: Anna! Tina! Hi!

(ANNA, *looking uncomfortable, seems disturbed by the* SALE *signs.*)

ANNA: Hey!

KATHERINE: How are you!

ANNA: Great, how are you?

KATHERINE: Oh good—you know, I haven't seen you in ages.

ANNA: Ah, well, I was in Bali.

KATHERINE: Oh. Well, how was that?

ANNA: Oh, God, it was—well, it's five thousand to get there, but, you know, they have these massages on the beach, three dollars and you just wake up feeling reborn.

You know I was telling Tina, it was like every sunrise was like the creation of the world. I mean it was truly the most spiritual place I've ever been.

KATHERINE: Wow. You should have come in before you left; we had some wonderful kind of sarcastic resort dresses.

ANNA: Oh, did you. Oh well, next time.

KATHERINE: Well, you know, why don't you come in now? Take advantage of the sale before the prices go back up.

ANNA: Um, well . . . I think we really have to run.

TINA: But we'll see you at the party tonight, won't we?

KATHERINE: Party?

TINA: At Anna's.

KATHERINE: Are you having a party tonight?

TINA: Whoops.

(ANNA *leans into* KATHERINE, *and almost whispers.*)

ANNA: Well, um, listen, Katherine, I'm sorry. It's just that, you know these days . . . it makes us nervous, somebody else's . . . well, you know . . . somebody else's troubles. I just need to be honest with you about that.

(KATHERINE *nods.* ANNA *and* TINA *walk away.* PETER *drifts out of the store. We can't hear them, but they are saying this:*)

KATHERINE: Oh, God. We have to get some money, fast.

PETER: We're doing the best that we can.

KATHERINE: No, we have to sell something. We have to sell the Ruscha.

PETER: No!

KATHERINE: We paid seventy-five, we can get one hundred fifty, maybe even one hundred sixty.

PETER: No!

KATHERINE: YES!! We have to sell it.

(*Now we can hear them.*)

PETER: I'm not selling that painting! Stop screaming!

KATHERINE: We're selling something. We've got to sell it.

PETER: No, I'll get it from my father.

KATHERINE: Oh, please, please. He will *never* give you the money.

PETER: That's a really original thought, you should write it down.

EXTERIOR: JEFF'S HOUSE. NIGHT.

A modern house, not too large, but a gem, in the Hollywood Hills. PETER *walks around the pool, the city sparkling below. He walks through the patio door; his father meets him.*

PETER: Hiya, Dad.

JEFF: Come in, come in. (JEFF *looks old, tired.*) How's the store?

PETER: It's dying, Dad.

JEFF: Well, you'll think of something.

PETER: What?

JEFF: I don't know.

(They have come into the living room; the fireplace is lit. On the couch is HILLY, *the saleswoman.)*

HILLY: Hello, Peter.

PETER: Am I interrupting something, Dad?

HILLY: No, not at all.

JEFF: Peter, could you come back tomorrow?

*(*PETER *looks at the scene and lurches away, back outside.* JEFF *calls after him.)*

JEFF: Peter! Come back, Peter! Fuck.

*(*PETER *stops, trudges back to him.)*

JEFF: You need money, don't you?

PETER: Times are hard right now, Dad.

JEFF: How much do you need?

PETER: A million dollars, but I'd settle for twenty thousand.

JEFF: Just give me a minute.

*(*JEFF *goes out for his checkbook.* PETER *looks at* HILLY.)*

PETER: Hi, Hilly. How's business?

HILLY: Great.

*(*JEFF *comes back with a check.)*

JEFF: Here you go.

PETER: Ten thousand dollars, Dad?

(PETER *starts to leave.*)

JEFF: You don't want it.

PETER: I do.

JEFF: Now, say thank you, son.

(PETER *returns, hugs* JEFF.)

PETER: Thank you, Dad. I'm sorry. Thanks.

(PETER *leaves.* JEFF *returns to* HILLY.
On the check.)

INTERIOR: HIPOCRACY. DAY.

On the check: it is in Katherine's hand. She is on the phone. PETER
watches her.

KATHERINE: Stonehurst National Bank? I'm calling to see if
a check that's been made out to us is any good? The
account number is—0697—24813 . . . Ten thousand dol-
lars . . . yes . . . Thank you.

PETER: Well?

(*She tears up the check.* PETER *is devastated.*)

INTERIOR: AUCTION HOUSE. DAY.

On the Ruscha. Gavel down.

AUCTIONEER: Sold!

INTERIOR: YOGA ROOM. DAY.

A long ommm. KATHERINE *and* SARAH, *as the class breaks up.*

SARAH: Namaste. Don't forget the drumming circle to-
night. So if you want to come, there's a flyer with all the
directions over there. Katherine! You should come.

KATHERINE: Yeah. Um, I have a date. It's a man.

SARAH: Well, you can't bring a man.

KATHERINE: No . . . well, I can't break the date.

SARAH: Well, it's your decision. And you'll do what you
have to do. But, just in case you change your mind, here,
the directions.
KATHERINE: Thanks.
(KATHERINE *takes the flyer from* SARAH.)

INTERIOR: WOMEN'S STEAM ROOM. DAY.
*The screen is filled with steam. Bodies appear, women: Asian, Anglo,
Black, old, young.* ALISON. *A woman pulls a towel off her face.*
KATHERINE.
KATHERINE: You're here?
ALISON: Yes.
KATHERINE: Alone?
ALISON: No.

INTERIOR: MEN'S JACUZZI. DAY.
PETER *and* MISHA, *side by side.*
PETER: How's business on the street?
MISHA: These are tough times. Tough, tough times.
PETER: Yeah.
(*An attendant comes in and hands the men slips of paper.
There is a mix-up; they exchange slips.*)

INTERIOR: MASSAGE ROOM AREA. DAY.
KATHERINE, ALISON, PETER, *and* MISHA *are each on a table, their rooms
divided by white muslin curtains. They melt into their massages.* ALI-
SON *speaks.*
ALISON: Peter?
PETER: Yes?
KATHERINE: Hi, Peter.
MISHA: Hi, everyone.
PETER: Hi, Katherine. Hello, Misha. What, Alison?
ALISON: I think it has to be over between us. I don't like
going out with a married man.

PETER: But I'm not married.

ALISON: Yes, you are.

PETER: No, I'm not.

ALISON: Are you divorced?

KATHERINE: Not yet.

PETER: Not yet.

ALISON: You live in the same house, you run a business together. Peter, I think you're married.

KATHERINE: But he is available.

ALISON: Katherine, did you know that Peter and I had been having an affair?

KATHERINE: No, I didn't, Alison.

ALISON: I thought you did.

PETER: You knew.

KATHERINE: I suspected.

ALISON: That it was me?

KATHERINE: No.

PETER: I thought you did.

KATHERINE: Nope. Not Alison. I didn't think she was your type. I always thought you'd go for someone taller.

ALISON: Do you think of yourself as married?

PETER: Who?

ALISON: Katherine.

KATHERINE: No. Yes. Technically.

ALISON: But you're with someone else now.

KATHERINE: Right.

ALISON: Well, how does he feel about it?

MISHA: Dirty, very dirty.

PETER: So what does this mean?

MISHA: Who?

PETER: Alison.

ALISON: It means . . . it means . . . I need to call a cab.

(ALISON *gets up. The massages continue. Now there are three bodies, four Korean masseurs.*)

KATHERINE: Misha?

MISHA: Yes, Katherine?

KATHERINE: I don't want to be with any men right now. Good night.

(KATHERINE *gets up, leaving the two men.*)

EXTERIOR: RESTAURANT. NIGHT.

PETER *is driving.* BETTINA *and a friend, the* OTHER KATHERINE, *are in front of a restaurant.* PETER *lowers the passenger window, and they talk to him.*

PETER: What luck.

BETTINA: This is my friend Katherine. Katherine, this is Peter.

PETER (*trying to keep alive*): So, what are you guys up to now?

BETTINA: We were going to a party tonight.

PETER: A party.

BETTINA: I'm not sure it's your kind of crowd.

PETER: What's my kind of crowd?

OTHER KATHERINE: The repressed.

BETTINA: That's not fair. It's just . . .

OTHER KATHERINE: It's going to be the usual art and spirituality and S&M crowd.

PETER: Whatever gets you through the night.

OTHER KATHERINE: Really? Whatever gets you through the night?

PETER: Get in.

(*Cut to:*)

EXTERIOR: SANTA MONICA MOUNTAINS. NIGHT.

In the distance, we hear drumming. KATHERINE *walks down a torch-lit trail until she reaches a clearing. Below her, she sees a circle of women lit by torches and candles.* SARAH *is in the middle of the circle, standing over a woman kneeling on the ground.* SARAH *blows on the woman's chest and head, then shakes a rattle. The woman sits still. Then* SARAH *waves her hand. The drums stop.*

SARAH: Katherine, are you ready?

(*Cut to:*)

* * *

INTERIOR/EXTERIOR: PARTY HOUSE. NIGHT.

We start in the foyer by a bed of nails, where VICTORIA *talks to some-one else:*

> VICTORIA: The problem with him is that he's still really just a swinger, and he pretends to be bisexual, but he comes to the parties, and all he does is try to make it with the women.

(PETER, BETTINA, *and the* OTHER KATHERINE *walk behind them, and then we pick up their conversation as they stroll through the house and around the pool. About thirty people, just as the* OTHER KATHER-INE *described them: the art and spirituality and S&M crowd. Art tat-toos [no Harley Davidsons], piercings.)*

> BETTINA: You know what goes on here?
>
> PETER: I can handle it.
>
> BETTINA: Nobody can handle it; that's why they need it.
>
> PETER: What are we talking about? What are we saying?
>
> BETTINA: It's secret stuff. The truth.

(*The women disappear.* PETER *is alone. He wanders. He passes an alcove where a group in leather watch a woman service a man in a sling. Then he overhears* BOB *talking casually to a few tattooed friends in a room with an extravagant buffet.)*

> BOB: Everyone here has a question. You wouldn't be here if you didn't have a question. And the only way to get the answer to your questions, the answer to questions you didn't even know you had, is through the body. You don't need anything else. All you need is the body. All the answers are there, inside you.
>
> NAKED MAN: Bob, does this mean we don't have to think—about anything?

(*The women reappear.*)

> BETTINA: Do you understand this?
>
> PETER: No.
>
> OTHER KATHERINE: Yes, you do.

(*Cut to:*)

* * *

EXTERIOR: SANTA MONICA MOUNTAINS. NIGHT.

SARAH *begins the ritual. She passes a feather around* KATHERINE, *and then some sage incense, wafting the smoke over Katherine's body.* KATHERINE *sits there.*

EXTERIOR: PARTY HOUSE. NIGHT.

PETER *sees* BETTINA *slide into the water. The light in the pool is beautiful, and the bodies are dark in it, shadows. The men have tattoos and nipple rings. Bettina has a few small tattoos, Kwakiutl birds on her shoulders, and nipple rings with a chain connecting them. She seems blissfully happy.* PETER *is the only one there still fully dressed.* PETER *drifts along the edge of the pool eating from a bowl of food.*

> BETTINA: Peter. Come in.
>
> PETER: In a minute.
>
> BETTINA: The water's warm.
>
> PETER: It's funny how people connect, isn't it?
>
> BETTINA: Another line. After the morals question.
>
> PETER: It isn't a line.
>
> BETTINA: It is a line.

(PETER *lies down next to the pool.*)

> PETER: No, but it's true. There is a connection between us. Something sparked, you know that.
>
> BETTINA: Sure, but it happens a lot though, you can't give into it every time.
>
> PETER: Why not? You have to trust your instincts.
>
> BETTINA: What are your instincts now?

(*Her smile: she relents: if he wants to kiss her, he can.*)

> PETER: My instincts?

(*He tries to kiss her; she pulls back.*)

> BETTINA: If you want to do that, you have to take off your pants.
>
> PETER: Yeah? I'm a little too shy.
>
> BETTINA: It's only a hard-on, Peter. Everyone here knows what they look like.

(*The* OTHER KATHERINE *swims up beside* BETTINA. PETER *stands up.*)

> OTHER KATHERINE: What were you guys talking about?
>
> BETTINA: Group sex.

OTHER KATHERINE: Oh, that. Really? What did he have in mind?

PETER: I'm not sure.

OTHER KATHERINE (*having fun, or does she mean it?*): Wouldn't you love to do us both?

PETER: Well.

BETTINA: You mean you wouldn't?

OTHER KATHERINE: Give us some details. Everyone has a detail or two worked out; what are yours?

PETER: I can play this game. (*He lies back down beside the pool.*) I was thinking we could go to a Japanese hotel.

OTHER KATHERINE: What's wrong with right here?

PETER: Well, you can't get room service here, no sushi.

BETTINA: A Japanese hotel?

PETER: Yeah, we'll get a suite. I'll pay.

BETTINA: Oooh, he'll pay, he'll pay. Fuzzy towels.

OTHER KATHERINE: Our own hot tub.

PETER: We could have fun.

OTHER KATHERINE (*to herself, not really meaning it, doesn't want to go*): With enough condoms . . .

PETER: I got them.

BETTINA (*decisively*): No. Not with Katherine, she's not my type. Besides, she's already going out with one married man.

OTHER KATHERINE (*laughing*): Yeah, and the hotel part, I don't know, it's sort of creepy, what are we, tourists?

PETER: Well, anyway, I was just kidding.

BETTINA: Right.

PETER: You were kidding too, right?

BETTINA: I was?

(*A* SWIMMER *enters frame behind the women. He is young and beautiful, and he smiles at* PETER, *close to his face.*)

SWIMMER: Why don't you stop talking so much and come in the water.

PETER: No.

SWIMMER: What are you afraid of? Just get undressed and come in the water.

PETER: How far does it go?

SWIMMER: We can't tell you that.

BETTINA: There's no shame here, Peter.

PETER: I'm scared.

SWIMMER (*with a comforting wink*): Because it's scary.

BETTINA: We'll be waiting.

(*They swim away. As* PETER *starts to leave, a tattooed man comes out another door.* VICTORIA *attends to* BOB, *who lies on a bed of nails. The mood of the scene changes, becomes serious.* PETER *can't watch. He leaves.*)

EXTERIOR: SANTA MONICA MOUNTAINS. NIGHT.

SARAH *dances around* KATHERINE, *and dramatizes what she sees. The women drummers never break their trance.*

SARAH: My spirit animals come to me, help me down into the lower world. To find that part of Katherine that is hurting, that is trapped. Help me down into the tunnel that is clogged with earth and roots and worms. I claw my way through. I emerge into a huge cave. Ohh! A huge bottle in space floating, Katherine is in it, up to her ears in blood and tears.

(KATHERINE *stands up, distraught.* SARAH *collapses into the hands of one of the other women.*)

KATHERINE: Shit! I'm sorry. I don't feel anything. You know, I can't fucking feel anything! (*She hits her head.*) Sarah! I can't feel anything, I'm . . . shit! shit!

EXTERIOR: SANTA MONICA MOUNTAINS. DAWN.

The sun is just coming up. KATHERINE *sees where she is, high on a ridge looking down at the coast.*

INTERIOR: LYLE'S ROOM. DAY.

KATHERINE *stands by the dresser.* LYLE *is in bed. He is very sick now.*

KATHERINE: I've been up all night, I just watched the sunrise.

LYLE: Was it nice?

KATHERINE: No. (*She crosses to him.*) How are you?

LYLE: How are you?

(*A gesture.* KATHERINE *is near tears. A silence.*)

LYLE: We're worried about you. We've all been worried about you.

(*She offers the same gesture. This makes them both smile, but neither laughs.*)

LYLE: How's Hipocracy?

KATHERINE: The store? (*The same gesture. Then she starts to cry. Silently, wracked.*) Umm. Well, I don't know. Uh, my life . . . my life, my life . . .

(LYLE *takes her hand.*)

EXTERIOR: POOL. NIGHT.

KATHERINE *stands alone by the pool. We move up to find* PETER *in a window, looking down. He turns away, and she leaves the pool.*

INTERIOR: PETER AND KATHERINE'S HOUSE. NIGHT.

PETER *in the living room.* KATHERINE *comes in. This is wordless. They test the line between them. They need each other, but they hate each other, but they love each other. The test is not to talk, not to say anything, to feel the silence between them. They walk around the house in a kind of dance. He leads her; he stops to see if she will come closer; she turns; he follows. And they are just inches away from each other, painfully close. And here, in the dark house at night, they make love. The passion is unrestrained, and they are equals.*

EXTERIOR: HIPOCRACY. DAY.

Painted on the outside window: EVERYTHING MUST GO!

INTERIOR: HIPOCRACY. DAY.

KATHERINE *and* PETER *sit together on a couch. They are drained.*

KATHERINE: We're three months behind in the mortgage payments on the house. We're going to be foreclosed.

(PETER *stares into space.*)

KATHERINE: Peter, we're going to lose the house. We have to do something. We have to change something.

PETER: I feel like killing myself. I really feel like killing myself. It's not a joke. I'm completely confused, I don't know what to do. We're going to fail. I don't see any way out.

KATHERINE: We have to hold onto life.

PETER: Why? Laura killed herself.

KATHERINE: Laura! Laura, Laura was in pain. She was *dying* in pain.

PETER: I am in pain. I'm in pain. Every second. I was born for no reason, my life has been just another life, and why can't I go the way she went? Why can't I just check out, maybe lose a little karma for it, but come back again as a tree or something and then work my way back up the ladder? Maybe I'm being punished in this life for some shit in my past, maybe I'm supposed to die now. Maybe death is calling me. That's what it feels like. There's a voice, it's the Angel of Death, and he's saying, here, I'm your friend, join me. Don't you hear that voice?

KATHERINE: You haven't earned your death.

PETER: Don't you hear that voice?

KATHERINE: No.

PETER: You're lying. You are lying.

KATHERINE: Sometimes.

PETER: Right. Sometimes.

KATHERINE: Everybody does.

PETER: Not the way we do, no. We're a little closer. I bet your fantasy is pretty well worked out, too. I bet you know exactly what you're going to wear.

KATHERINE (*after a long pause*): Well, I know it isn't black. Black is too obvious. Something summery, June wedding, a print, flowers. But elegant. For the evening, not the afternoon. How about you?

(*Two men come into the store. They interrupt the conversation be-tween* KATHERINE *and* PETER *when indicated.*)

PETER: Well, I had been thinking about black tie, but you make a good point.

KATHERINE: You don't want to go out looking like a head-waiter.

PETER: No, it's true, but the stylish young president of a big foundation, that's sort of romantic.

(*The* CUSTOMERS *pick out a gray sweater and take it to the counter.* PETER *and* KATHERINE *follow them there.*)

CUSTOMER #1: Yeah, that should work. Terry'd look pretty good in a thing like this, don't you think?

CUSTOMER #2: Terry'd look awesome.

CUSTOMER #1: What do you mean by that?

CUSTOMER #2: What do you mean, what do I mean by that? She'd look good in it, that's what I mean.

PETER (*to* KATHERINE *as they approach the counter*): Really? What are you going to do when the store fails?

KATHERINE: I'll get a job. Maybe I'll learn massage.

PETER (*to the* CUSTOMERS): Cash or charge?

CUSTOMER #1: Plastic. Seventy percent off, right?

(*He hands* PETER *his card.*)

KATHERINE (*in response to the customer's question*): Yes. (*Continuing with* PETER:) Homelessness is a possibility, I know that.

PETER: Homeless. Sleeping in our car. Washing up in the bathroom at a library. Eating out of garbage cans. That could happen to us.

KATHERINE: It doesn't have to.

PETER: The people living on the streets, Katherine, weren't born on the street. This is how it happens: you just keep on falling; there's no bottom. Do you think the Navajos just had children whenever they wanted to?

KATHERINE: What are you talking about?

PETER: We were all born because the economy was ex-panding. See, now it's collapsing. The world doesn't need us. In the old days, the laws of nature kept everything in balance, when people were in harmony with nature. And now, nature is dead, and there's no more harmony, and we're all pointless. (*To the* CUSTOMERS, *with charm:*) Will that be all?

CUSTOMER #1: Yeah.

PETER (*smiling, as though the* CUSTOMERS *haven't heard a word he has said*): Great.

(*The card has been approved, and the receipt printed out.* PETER *tears it off, and* CUSTOMER #1 *signs.*)

CUSTOMER #1: Thanks.

CUSTOMER #2: Yeah, thanks a lot.

KATHERINE: I'm going to Lone Pine for a few days. I need some air.

(*The telephone rings. It is another phone* SALESMAN [*voice-over*].)

PETER: Hello?

SALESMAN (*voice-over*): Hello. Is this Peter Witner?

PETER: Who's calling?

SALESMAN (*voice-over*): May I speak to Peter Witner?

PETER: Are you a salesman?

SALESMAN (*voice-over*): You're probably saying that because you've had a bad experience with salesmen, isn't that right, Peter Witner?

PETER: And you just had a bad experience with a customer. (*He hangs up. To* KATHERINE:) I'm coming with you.

KATHERINE: No. Peter.

PETER: Yes, yes, wait, wait—

KATHERINE: Please, no.

(*She runs out.*)

EXTERIOR: HIPOCRACY. DAY.

He chases her; she runs from him.

PETER: Please, please, Katherine. You're all I have. I'm all you have. Please.

KATHERINE: Peter.

(*Fade-out:*)

*   *   *

EXTERIOR: LONE PINE. DESERT. DAY.

A staggering vista: the desert, the sky, the rocks. And a circle of stones about forty feet across.

    ELLEN: This is a sacred spot. This is one of those places where the Earth's energy is concentrated.

    KATHERINE: Do you feel it?

    PETER: Oh, sure . . . It's great.

(She gets it. He tries, but he doesn't really. PETER watches her. Everyone wanders, trying to grasp something. PETER tries.)

EXTERIOR: THE DESERT. NIGHT.

Everyone sits around a fire, looking at the stars.

    JEAN: If you listen, if you listen without just listening to something, you can hear the silence. The silence in which we chose to be born, the silence in which we chose our parents, the silence in which we choose our lives. The silence in which we can choose our death.

    PETER: Choose our death?

    JEAN: To be born human and not a snake is a tremendous opportunity. Ask yourself, who wishes to die, who, for whom? Would your death be appropriate? Would your death be adequate? I will leave my answer open. But you should go to the end of your question. If you ever open another store, Peter, watch the location.

(PETER listens to this carefully, and KATHERINE watches him listening. When JEAN is finished: the stars and sparks from the fire rising toward them.)

EXTERIOR: DESERT. DAY.

KATHERINE *climbs up on a plateau. Others are nearby wandering. Then suddenly, there is a sandstorm, some sudden trick of nature. People cry out.*

JEAN: There's nothing you can do, so there's nothing to be afraid of.

(*And then all the people listen, which is all that they can do. All are obscured. They stand where they are. People are near each other, reach out for each other, but nobody touches. Everyone disperses.* ELLEN *sees* PETER *headed in the same direction she has.*)

ELLEN: Peter. Peter.

(PETER *reaches* ELLEN, *and they embrace. The storm clears a bit, and* KATHERINE *sees, in this moment of clarity,* PETER *and* ELLEN *leaning against a rock, groping each other. We can't tell what* KATHERINE *is thinking, but something has changed for her.* KATHERINE *watches her husband making out with another woman, and after a moment when the storm hides* PETER *and* ELLEN, *she runs into the storm; then we find her running across the open desert, away from everyone. She stops violently. And then she turns and walks back slowly. When we would expect rage, she smiles.*)

INTERIOR: HIPOCRACY. DAY.

It is cluttered, a bit like a junk shop.

Another montage: It's a Going out of Business Sale.

Finally, the store is empty. As PETER *and* KATHERINE *get ready to leave, the phone rings.* KATHERINE *answers it.*

KATHERINE: Hello?

SALESMAN (*voice-over*): Hello, may I speak to Peter Witner?

KATHERINE: It's for you.

(PETER *takes the phone.*)

PETER: Yeah?

SALESMAN (*voice-over*): Peter Witner?

PETER: Yeah.

SALESMAN (*voice-over*): Congratulations, you've been selected as a grand prize winner in a nationwide sweepstakes!

PETER: Where are you?

SALESMAN (*voice-over*): I'm sorry?

PETER: I need a job!

(*Cut to:*)

* * *

INTERIOR: NOVA MARKETING TRAINING ROOM. DAY.

PETER *and a few other trainees sit in chairs arranged in a circle.* DALE DEVEAUX *and* MR. COBORUBIEZ *stride into the room.*

> DALE: When's the last time anyone in this room had a real vacation? Come on, I want to know. Come on, come on, I really want to know.

(A hand raised.)

> WOMAN: I went back to Massachusetts to visit my parents last month.
> DALE: And who paid for the fucking ticket?
> WOMAN: My mother.
> DALE: I'm not talking about two weeks in Pittsfield! That's not a vacation. I'm talking about . . . Acapulco, margaritas, sex! When was the last time you had sex in a good hotel room with the sound of the ocean outside? When was the last time you ordered room service? I did, last week. Anybody else?

*(*DALE *knocks over a grandfather clock. Four feet tall and it must weigh three pounds. It breaks apart on the floor. The chimes and chains are plastic; the clock itself is driven by a single AA battery.)*

> DALE: And Mr. Coborubiez was in the next room, and he was getting laid. Ain't that right, Mr. Coborubiez? . . . This job is about making money. You're going to get on those phones, and you're going to remember that the person you are selling to is a thief, and I can prove he's a thief. He's a thief, because he has your money! And you're going to do everything you can to get your money back.

INTERIOR: LAURA AND LYLE'S HOUSE. DAY.

KATHERINE *runs up the stairs of their empty house. She is frantic. She goes to the medicine chest in the bathroom. She finds the bottles of sedatives. She puts the bottle in her bag. She leaves.*

* * *

INTERIOR: NOVA MARKETING TRAINING ROOM. DAY.

DALE *picks up a binder.*

> DALE: This is your script. Every possible objection anyone can have to the pitch is in this script. You're going to get down into these phones, you have to visualize yourself standing there in the little pet store, in that little yogurt store, in that little flower shop, you have to see yourself making friends with them, talking to them, stroking them, so confident of yourself and of the lie you're telling that you get radioactive, you start to glow! Why? So they'll do what you want them to do. And what is it that you want them to do? You want Mom and Pop America to reach down into their pockets, pull out their wallets, and read you the number off their credit card. And when you have that . . . you'll have something far more precious than my respect. You'll have your money.

INTERIOR: NOVA MARKETING. DAY.

PETER *is in the phone room. A row of booths lines three walls of the room. Each salesman is sitting with a stack of phone books, Yellow Pages.* PETER *is on the phone.*

> VOICE: Hav-a-Heart.
>
> PETER: Uh, yes. Hello, this Bob Dobbs. May I, is this— (*checks the Yellow Pages*) the Tale of the Dog pet shop?
>
> VOICE: Yes, it is.
>
> PETER: Is this the owner, uh?
>
> VOICE: Just a second.
>
> PETER: Yes, my name is Robert Dobbs, congratulations, you're the grand prize winner in a nation—

(*And* PETER *hears the owner of Tale of the Dog slam the receiver down.* DALE *comes up behind* PETER.)

> PETER: Shit.
>
> DALE: Don't you wish you'd gone to med school?

(PETER *tries again. This time he dials from the White Pages.*)

> VOICE: *Hola!*
>
> PETER: Hello? Yes. Congratulates, uh, uh, congratulations, uh.

VOICE: *Que?*

PETER: *Habla usted Ingles?*

(PETER *gives up.* DALE *comes up behind him again.*)

DALE: Does it bother you that the only prize they're ever going to win is that clock?

(PETER *becomes resolved. He grabs a phone book and dials the number for Bloomin' Love, a flower shop in Burlington, Vermont. A woman answers,* SANDI REGO. PETER *closes his eyes. An image appears: a flower arrangement, superimposed on his face. He opens his eyes, and in the mirror in front of him, he sees* SANDI REGO *in her flower shop.* PETER *talks to her, smiling, and then we are in.*)

SANDI REGO: Hello?

PETER: May I speak to the owner, please?

SANDI REGO: Speaking.

PETER: Hello, this is Bob Dobbs, vice-president of marketing here at the Nova Corporation. Congratulations, you're a grand prize winner in a nationwide contest.

SANDI REGO: Oh, my God! I've never won anything.

PETER: Well, you have now—uh, Sandi Rego, yes! You've been selected as a grand prize winner in a nationwide contest, and you've won either a . . . a trip to Hawaii, all expenses paid—

SANDI REGO: Hawaii!

INTERIOR: BLOOMIN' LOVE FLOWERS. DAY.

And PETER *is at the counter, talking to* SANDI REGO. *Or rather,* PETER *is half there, his image ghostly, a mirage.*

PETER: Or a complete Mitsubishi home entertainment system, worth: fifteen thousand dollars!

SANDI REGO: Can I have the trip to Hawaii instead?

INTERIOR: NOVA MARKETING. DAY.

PETER *is back in the room, looking at the script around him, reading from an objection card marked* CAN I HAVE THE TRIP INSTEAD? PETER *reads the answer.*

PETER: Well, it wouldn't be a contest if we could tell you which prize you'd won, would it . . .

SANDI REGO: Roger, we won some sort of contest. (*To* PETER:) So what else?

PETER: Or you might have won a—an authentic heirloom quality grandfather clock.

(*He looks at the clock, this piece of shit. Then he goes back into himself, back into the flower store.*)

SANDI REGO: What do I have to do?

PETER: We're running a special offer this month on personally imprinted pens.

SANDI REGO: Oh, I don't think I need any pens.

PETER: Do you need that trip to Hawaii?

SANDI REGO: Oh, I could use that.

PETER: Well, what color would you like on those pens, Sandi?

(*Peter's image gets stronger through this speech until he is fully in his vision of the flower store, until he is there.*)

SANDI REGO: Well, how much are they?

PETER: One hundred forty-nine dollars, plus shipping and handling.

SANDI REGO: Maybe I should wait until my husband gets back. I better ask him.

(*Peter's image abruptly fades from the store. He collects himself, concentrates, and speaks again.*)

PETER: Look, um, Sandi Reg—Sandi, can we—let's cut to—let's speak frankly. You know, Sandy, I was speaking with a woman in Arizona, quite like yourself, an entrepreneur, she owned a pet shop, and she said the same thing to me, she said I better wait for my husband. And I said ma'am, wouldn't you really like it to be a surprise, I mean, if you really love him, wouldn't you like to surprise him, with that Hawaiian vacation, that entertainment system, that *beautiful* grandfather clock, wouldn't you?

SANDI REGO: God, you're a good salesman.

PETER (*radioactive*): And the credit card number?

(SANDI REGO *reaches for her credit cards and slowly selects the right one.*)

    SANDI REGO: 9427-708-9831.

(PETER *is now a blinding white light.*)

    PETER: Great, Sandi, your surprise is on its way.

    SANDI REGO: Oh, my God! You know, I have never won anything.

    PETER: Well, you have now.

    DALE (*behind him*): Wait for the hang up.

(SANDI REGO *hangs up. The vision disappears.* PETER *hangs up.*)

    DALE: This is a man! Ladies and gentlemen, have you ever seen a man? This is a man!

(PETER *stands up as everyone cheers him. They applaud. He walks through the crowd, faster, to escape, to the door.*)

INTERIOR: PETER AND KATHERINE'S HOUSE. DAY.

PETER *comes in. He is defeated, exhausted. The piano is playing Beethoven. Votive candles line the hallway to the bedroom, past the dinosaurs.*

INTERIOR: PETER AND KATHERINE'S BEDROOM. DAY.

    PETER: Katherine? Katherine? Katherine, I have wonderful news. I don't think we have to sell the house. You see I had a great success today, and I think everything is going to be all right. I bullshitted an old lady in a flower shop, ninety-eight cents worth of pens for a hundred and forty-nine bucks and a five-dollar clock that would just . . . float away if it didn't have a battery to weigh it down, so she's going to pay eighty dollars in shipping costs because she thinks she's won it as a prize. That's what I did today. And I did it brilliantly. And I'm one of those guys now.

(*He looks around. Everything is clean. There is hardly any furniture, no art.*)

    PETER: Katherine? (*Again, louder.*) Katherine?

(*Her voice:*)

KATHERINE: Don't turn around. There's your suit. I'll be downstairs. Maybe you should take a shower. And pour yourself a drink. It's a pitcher of margaritas. I thought of champagne, but, you know, sometimes the bubbles are just so obvious. Tequila is so Mexican, so Day of the Dead.

(*The suit hangs in an otherwise empty closet. And there is the pitcher on a tray with two glasses.*

PETER *pours himself a drink as he starts to undress. He relaxes.*)

INTERIOR: LIVING ROOM. DAY.

PETER *comes out, beautifully groomed.*

The room is empty now except for the player piano and the piano bench. A silver-domed tray sits on the bench. The piano continues to play.

PETER: Katherine?

(KATHERINE *appears behind him.*)

KATHERINE: Here I am.

(*He spins around.*)

PETER: Wow.

(*She looks beautiful, exquisite, in a ten-thousand-dollar gown.*)

KATHERINE: When you're calling on the Angel of Death, you have to call in style, don't you think?

(*She lifts the silver dome. Two beautiful bowls, two beautiful spoons, and yogurt. She looks* PETER *in the eye.* PETER *picks up the bowls, and* KATHERINE *chooses one.*)

PETER: May I propose a toast?

KATHERINE: Of course.

PETER (*with a brave smile*): Till death do us part. (*Beat.*) I can only do this if you know that I love you. Do you know that? Do you know that I love you?

KATHERINE: I know that.

(*He takes it to his mouth and then swallows the yogurt, and looking her in the eye, takes another, and another. A bit drips on his chin, and she wipes it off with a napkin. Then, with a mysterious little smile, she takes hers. He gives himself another spoon and makes a face.*)

PETER: Hmm!

KATHERINE: Bitter?

PETER: Yeah . . .

KATHERINE: I'm sorry.

PETER: Don't apologize.

KATHERINE: Sweetener?

PETER: Sugar. What the hell, let's live dangerously.

(*She goes to the kitchen.*

Now the piano is playing something new: it is what ALISON *played that night at the house when* KATHERINE *was with* MISHA.

We see the traces of her hands, and then we see where she missed a key as PETER *kissed her. We see the outlines of Alison's elbows as she turned around, and the notes wiped as they brushed against the keyboard.*

KATHERINE *returns from the kitchen.* PETER *is ashamed of himself.*)

PETER: I'm sorry if I ever hurt you.

(KATHERINE *offers him a hand, with a smile.*)

KATHERINE: Peter, that's all finished now. It's over . . . Now
. . . shall we go?

(*She leads him to the bedroom, past the votive candles.*)

INTERIOR: PETER AND KATHERINE'S BEDROOM. DAY.

Into the bedroom.

KATHERINE: I'm feeling a bit . . . light-headed right now.

PETER: Katherine, baby, my feet are cold.

KATHERINE: Mmm.

(*She lies down on the bed, and he joins her. Her eyes are closed.*)

PETER: Katherine?

KATHERINE: Uh?

PETER: That's all I feel. My feet are freezing.

KATHERINE: Uh.

PETER (*groggy*): Kath, is it, enough stuff—

KATHERINE: Huh?

PETER: Katherine, did you do enough stuff . . . in mine?

KATHERINE: Huh?

PETER: There it is.

KATHERINE: Mmmm.

PETER: This isn't so bad. Hello. Hello, Mr. Death. Kath—
(*He lifts a hand to stroke her head, but he can't. His hand falls. When it does, she sits up slowly and looks at him, passing a hand over his eyes. A slight blink.*)

KATHERINE: Peter?
(*Hardly any response, his breath is forced and shallow. She passes a hand in front of his eyes again, and now we see her from his point of view. She is looking down at him.*

PETER *fights to get one last breath out, one last word.*)

PETER: Yeah . . . what . . . what is this?
(*And we see* KATHERINE *from his point of view. She holds up Lyle's medicine bottle. She is gentle with* PETER.)

KATHERINE: It's a divorce. You'll wake up in three or four hours. If you really want to kill yourself, there's enough left in here to do it. But it's your choice. I don't want to murder you.

(*She gives the bottle to him. She kisses his forehead.*)

KATHERINE: I want to live.

PETER: Katherine—
(PETER *collapses into his drugged sleep.* KATHERINE *walks away, taking off her gloves.*

On PETER: *he is on the bed, one last time.*

Back to KATHERINE: *she walks away, down the hall, lit by the votive candles.*

Dissolve to:)

INTERIOR: EYEGLASS STORE. DAY.
A magnificent floral arrangement and our first thought must be: this is a funeral. The source music is a funeral chorale.

KATHERINE *steps into the frame, looking serious. Is she mourning? She lifts a watering can and tends the flowers.*

The music changes; now we hear "Besame Mucho," the same song that Jeff was playing when Peter asked him for money.

KATHERINE *looks back, and we move with her and discover that we are in an elegant eyeglass store. An employee works with customers. Another employee eats lunch in a back alcove.* KATHERINE *arranges eyeglasses on a display case. It has been one year. We zoom in to look at her. She turns. We hear a voice.*

>WOMAN: I went to Cleveland last month to see my parents.

(*Smash cut to:*)

INTERIOR: NOVA MARKETING. DAY.

We see PETER. *He is training another cross section of the city.*

>PETER: And who paid for the fucking ticket? Cleveland is not a vacation! I'm talking about room service. I'm talking about sex with someone new. Listen to me, because I know where you've been, and I'm here to tell you that your life is in your hands now. I'm here to tell you that you can live, or you can die. Did you know that in Chinese the word for *crisis* is the same as the word for *opportunity?* Did you know that?

(*Cut to:*)

BLACKNESS.

JEAN *enters frame.*

>JEAN: Live with the question.

(JEAN *leaves frame.*)